Education Tax Credits

And Other Educational Incentives

By Dana Bell, EA

Copyright

Send book feedback to edcredit@tylerhosting.com.

ISBN: 978-1-329-63782-5

Dana Bell, EA
607 Pam Drive
Tyler, Texas

Colophon

This book was created in LibreOffice Writer and converted by Adobe Acrobat to a gray-scale PDF for publication on demand. Software images were captured using the Microsoft HTML Help Image Editor. The cover was created in Photoshop CS4. The ePub and derivatives were created in Sigil.

About the Type

The text uses 12 point Gentium Basic, a typeface from SIL International, formerly Southern Institute of Linguistics. It is a variation of the original Gentium font designed by Victor Gaultney. The headings were set in Franklin Gothic Book.

Table of Contents

Alert

In the previously published Education Tax Credit Essentials I indicated that taxpayers do not have to have a 1098-T in order to claim an education credit. Following the passage of H. R. 1295 that will no longer be the case. The new law was passed June 29, 2015 as part of the Trade Preferences Extension Act of 2015 and adds the following as IRC § 25A(g)(8):

> *PAYEE STATEMENT REQUIREMENT.—Except as otherwise provided by the Secretary, no credit shall be allowed under this section unless the taxpayer receives a statement furnished under section 6050S(d) which contains all of the information required by paragraph (2) thereof.*

A similar requirement exists for the tuition deduction.

Note that the requirement does not take effect until the 2016 tax years for most individual taxpayers. A note in the bill Section 804(d) and the law (IRC § 25A) clarifies

> *Effective Date.--The amendments made by this section shall apply to taxable years beginning after the date of the enactment of this Act.*

While taxpayers will be required to have a 1098-T following 2016, institutions are often not required to provide one. Until that is remedied, many taxpayers could be deprived of an education credit or deduction they would have otherwise been qualified for. I anticipate that the IRS will issue new regulations to reconcile the discrepancy.

Preface

In 2014 the Department of Treasury released a 4-page document explaining in part, how taxpayers can coordinate their Pell grant with qualifying expenses to maximize their education credit. That document also has a section that explains how to help with the appeal to "inform students that they have a choice in how to allocate Pell Grants for tax purposes."

The IRS has been attempting to educate taxpayers on the subject of education tax credits and scholarship inclusion for years. Pub 970 has discussed this in the past, but now the encouragement has been added to the 8863 instructions and in 2015 will be included on the back of the 1098-T.

Not only do students need to be aware of the potential of Pell grants and educational expenses, so do their parents, educational institutions, financial planners, and tax professionals. While I am not responding to that particular appeal to inform others, I am using this text to try to encourage others, with a focus on tax professionals, to learn more about education tax credits.

Being Informed

Education credits were first introduced in 1998 but they have been expanded or extended three times. The AOTC is now good until 2017 but it will likely be extended or expanded again before that expiration.

Many tax professionals bemoan the complexity of education incentives but the biggest problem of taxpayers is being informed concerning education tax credits and other assistance. And it's not just that they don't have the information, much of the information that is being presented is wrong, grossly incomplete, or outdated. Getting tax professionals informed is thus the primary purpose of this book.

Lack of Information

One of the most popular sites for education-related information is www.1098-T.com, primarily because they deliver electronic versions of the 1098-T, the form often used to report expenses for the credit. The information provided on that site for the American Opportunity Tax Credit includes the statement,

> ... higher education expenses paid with a tax-free scholarship, Pell Grant or employer-provided educational assistance cannot be used when figuring your education credits. Eligible expenses for this credit are offset by scholarships, grants, and other tax-free tuition benefits.[1]

While this may be true, the lack of additional information makes this misleading.

Other sources of education credit information comes from big box tax chains like H&R Block[2] and TurboTax[3]. The mantra is that tax-free amounts you use to cover expenses cannot be used to claim the credits. That's true, but it's not the whole truth. These tax chains often employ minimally trained preparers, and focus on only the simplest and most basic returns, and routine credits like the EITC. Even if they knew, they may not know how to do it right.

Misinformation

This lack of information further leads to misinformation and one of the biggest sources of misinformation is from institutions. Treasury Regulations allow institutions to forego providing students a 1098-T when financial aid exceeds qualified expenses. That has led many institutions to believe that students do not qualify for an education credit in those cases. Tyler Junior College, our local junior college indicates that if you didn't get a 1098-T, you don't qualify for an education credit.

---

1   https://www.1098-T.com/info/tra97/trainfo_hope.asp
2   http://www.hrblock.com/tax-answers/services/jsp/article.jsp?
     article_id=67005
3   https://ttlc.intuit.com/questions/1901069-are-scholarships-fellowships-
     and-grants-considered-taxable-income

Outdated Information

Web resources that provide education credit information often include disclaimers that indicate that the information does not constitute tax advice, but many times the statements are grossly incomplete.

Not only is scholarship inclusion information not included but many sites only mention the Hope Scholarship which covers 2 years and have nothing about the American Opportunity Tax Credit (passed in 2008). One such site is collegeforalltexans.com (Copyright © 2015 Texas Higher Education Coordinating Board) which only lists the Hope Tax Credit.[4]

Mixed Signals

Sometimes you can get mixed signals from the same company or organization. Although information is often incomplete, incorrect, or outdated, there are cases where more accurate information is available from the same entity.

The IRS is well-known for giving conflicting advice. While instructions indicate taxpayers can include scholarships in income to increase education credits, not every IRS employee will tell you that. Even presenters in IRS webinars have used the argument that expenses must be paid out of pocket, though none of the IRS instructions include that requirement.

Many H&R Block sites will not know about scholarship re-characterization, but the Tax Institute at H&R Block does have it right at http://blogs.hrblock.com/2014/08/26/federal-student-aid-what-are-the-tax-consequences/, at least in reference to Pell grants.

Alternate Treatments

The latest obstacle to being informed about education tax credits is in the use of alternate treatments and interpretations. Entities are learning about the opportunities but are reluctant to take advantage

---

4   http://www.collegeforalltexans.com/apps/financialaid/tofa.cfm?
     Kind=TX, Accessed 9/19/2015.

of them, so they add additional restrictions as safeguards against inappropriate claims.

Meeting the Challenges

The theory of education credits is really simple. Taxpayers can earn a credit for amounts paid for qualifying expenses. The tax code and regulations concerning education tax credits are also relatively straightforward. In practice, however, education credits present a number of challenges. The first challenge is understanding how scholarships and grants come into play and the differences between scholarships. The second challenge is determining qualifying expenses as the document that contains that information may not be complete or accurate. Another challenge involves coordinating the tax credits with other benefits and other aspects of the tax return. The final challenge is educating clients about education credits. Educating clients may be the first step in the preparation, but professionals first need to have a firm grip on education credits and the many ramifications of financing education.

Book Outline

The goal of this text is to help you meet these challenges by enabling you to plan the process of calculating education credits. Following are the basics you need to know to prepare returns with education credits, tasks that I address in the first part of the book.

- Understanding the Education Credits
- Understanding the Regulations
- Researching Scholarships
- Document Preparation
- Student Account Tabulation
- Tax Credit Calculation

Additionally there are some suggestions for more efficient processes, effective strategies, and tax planning opportunities presented in the second part of the book.

- Tax Preparation Techniques
- Software Solutions
- Special Issues
- Documentation
- Planning and Coordination
- Amending for Education Credits

There are only two education credits under the current tax code and this book focuses primarily on the American Opportunity Tax Credit. Brief discussions of the Lifetime Learning Credit and various deductions are also included.

This text started as a series of articles on the blog Switched Keys describing how to claim education credits. The articles and other resources are also part of an AOTC toolkit that can be downloaded from www.tylerhosting.com/EdCredit/.

Additional Information

A prior edition of this book was published in May providing the above essentials needed to claim education credits. This is the expanded version of the text which includes additional fluff that may interest other readers.

This version of Education Tax Credits includes information on these other forms of educational assistance.

- Educational Savings Accounts (Section 529, Coverdell)
- IRAs used for educational expenses
- Employer-Provided Educational Assistance
- Financial Aid
- Student Loans

While tax credits and deductions may be popular among lower-income taxpayers, high-earning taxpayers are more likely to be interested in things like Section 529 and Coverdell savings accounts, so I've discussed them in more detail in this version. While tax credits can be claimed as an afterthought, these other tax incentives require a considerable amount of forethought.

General information is also presented on how to combine the different forms of educational assistance to optimize educational expenses. This version also closes with a look at the future of educational credits. Appendices include information on related topics such as my education credit campaign and a discussion of the TIGTA study of tax credits and suspected fraud.

Comments, questions, and corrections are welcome and can be submitted through the contact form on the blog, or directly to edcredit@tylerhosting.com. I have discovered a couple of issues during the writing and publishing process and I am sure I have omitted information that you might think useful and relevant. Let me know.

Information Requirement Unresolved

One thing that still remains unresolved concerning education credits is the reconciliation of new education credit requirements and the reporting requirements of educational institutions. Currently, taxpayers are generally not required to have a 1098-T in order to claim an education credit. For tax years starting after the passing of H. R. 1295, taxpayers are required to have this form in order to claim the credit.

> *(8) Payee statement requirement*
>
> *Except as otherwise provided by the Secretary, no credit shall be allowed under this section unless the taxpayer receives a statement furnished under section 6050S(d) which contains all of the information required by paragraph (2) thereof.*

A note clarifies the timing of this requirement as the tax year following enactment (Pub. L. 114–27, title VIII, § 804(d)).[5]

> *Effective Date.--The amendments made by this section shall apply to*

---

5   http://www.gpo.gov/fdsys/pkg/PLAW-114publ27/html/PLAW-114publ27.htm

taxable years beginning after the date of the enactment of this Act.

The difficulty is that currently institutions are not always required to provide the 1098-T. Individual taxpayers generally use a calendar year, so the effective date would be January 1, 2016 for returns due by April 15, 2017.

Reading Notes

Footnotes

Generally, footnotes are restricted to external sources other than references to the tax code or regulations. Links for most of the external websites are likewise included in the footnotes.

Tax Code and Regulations

Code sections and references to Treasury Regulations are generally provided in the text, usually at the end of relevant paragraphs, without any links to websites. Tax practitioners can read the tax code and regulations on the internet in several places. The tax code and treasury regulations are officially published by the GPO at http://www.gpo.gov/fdsys/search/home.action but they are also easily accessible from Cornell's **Legal Information Institute** website at https://www.law.cornell.edu.

Instead of navigating through the code, you can use the shortcut patterns for code sections and regulations.

For code sections, use the pattern

```
https://www.law.cornell.edu/uscode/text/26/<codesec>
```

For example, IRC § 25A would be accessed at

https://www.law.cornell.edu/uscode/text/26/25A

For Treasury Regulations, use the pattern

```
https://www.law.cornell.edu/cfr/text/26/<treasreg>
```

For example, Treas. Reg. § 1.25A-1 would be accessed at

https://www.law.cornell.edu/cfr/text/26/1.25A-1

Alternately, tax law can be viewed at http://uscode.house.gov/, and other sites.

Forms and Publications

IRS tax forms and publications can be accessed from the IRS website at http://www.irs.gov/Forms-&-Pubs.

The Basics

In the beginning Congress created deductions for educational expenses but taxpayers could only enjoy those deductions if certain rules were followed. Deductions were decreases in taxable income. If there was no taxable income, there was no benefit. At that time scholarships were considered tax-free if used for qualified expenses.

Then there were credits. In 1998 the Hope Scholarship Credit was established that allowed taxpayers to claim expenses that were paid for qualified educational expenses during the first two years of college. These credits reduced the actual tax that was due, rather than lower taxable income as deductions. Of course, if the taxpayer did not owe any tax then he could not reduce that tax. The related Lifetime Learning Credit was also available but none of it was refundable either.

Over the years changes were made to the available credits. In 2009 the American Recovery and Reinvestment Act enhanced the Hope Credit, giving it a new name, the American Opportunity Tax Credit. It also made a portion of it refundable allowing taxpayers to consider the credit as a payment, which could be refunded even if he did not owe any tax. In 2011, the credit was extended through 2012 by the Tax Relief and Job Creation Act of 2010. In 2012 the AOTC was extended through 2017 by the American Taxpayer Relief Act of 2012.

Overview

The American Opportunity Tax Credit (AOTC or AOC) allows taxpayers to get a credit for $4,000 of qualified educational expenses. The total credit could amount to $2,500 in tax reduction. The first $2,000 is a 100% credit and the second $2,000 is a 25% credit. Only 40% of the AOTC is refundable so the maximum refund without tax reduction is $1,000. The Lifetime Learning Credit (LLC) is a 20% credit for up to $10,000 of educational expenses to gain or improve job skills. None of the LLC is refundable.

Taxpayers must choose between the LLC and the AOTC however, as they cannot claim both credits for the same student. If either credit is used, the tuition deduction is not allowed for that student. You can, however, claim the AOTC for one student and the LLC for another. There are also phase-outs for both credits. Lower income taxpayers are likely to use the American Opportunity Credit since it does not require taxable income for the refundable part of the credit. Some of the rules for AOTC are that the student must have been at least half-time and seeking a recognized educational credential.

When you search the web for education credits, this is often all that you will find on many websites. In many cases, the website is so out of date that it may mention the Hope Credit instead of the American Opportunity Tax Credit, and refer to the first two years instead of the first four years of undergraduate study. Still, there are other aspects of the credits that are not well known. For example, the regulations allow students to include some of their scholarships in income to increase the credit. Very often that is not mentioned.

The Regulations section later discusses that treatment along with other ways to coordinate the many other education benefits that may be used. There is a maze of other educational benefits that are available which may be more advantageous depending on the taxpayer's income level, tax bracket and other circumstances. For example, if you are in the 25% marginal tax bracket then the AOTC or a deduction would probably be more advantageous than the 20% LLC. Many other circumstances could affect your decision as well.

Note: It has been said that the American Opportunity Tax Credit replaces the Hope Credit. That is only partially true. The rules for AOTC modify the requirements for the Hope Credit and are good through tax year 2017, but the Hope Credit is not limited in time. Unless Congress makes changes in the law the Hope Credit will still be good in 2018 and later.

What You Need to Know

What you need to know about education credits will depend on who you are. The IRS categorizes knowledge requirements for schools,

1098-T filers, and tax preparers. If the taxpayer is preparing their own return they would be the tax preparer. The IRS web page provides a summary of those "need to know" facts at http://www.eitc.irs.gov/Other-Refundable-Credits/aotcllc.

This text is primarily focused on what the tax preparer needs to know about the education credits to prepare returns and provide advice to clients. However, the client needs to know enough about education credits to see the benefits of providing the preparer the necessary information. The primary "need to know" facts include qualifications, qualifying expenses, and qualifying payments. The sections following discuss those elements for the credits.

Preparers will also need to gather relevant taxpayer information from client-provided documents or through the interview process. Additionally, an understanding of 1098-T information and limitations is crucial to preparing accurate returns.

American Opportunity Tax Credit

Qualifications

Separate qualifications for the AOTC relate to the taxpayer and the student. The taxpayer (often a parent) must be claiming a dependency exemption for the student in order to claim the AOTC. Students qualifying for the AOTC can be any dependent for which you are allowed to take a dependency exemption (IRC § 25A(f)(1)(A)(iii)), including individuals that meet the test for dependency exemption as a qualifying relative. So, it's possible to claim the credit for a student who is a parent or a person whom you support and who lives with you all year (IRC § 152).

If the taxpayer is the student, he must not be claimed by someone else. One of the pitfalls of the taxpayer qualifications is that a married student must file a joint return in order for the taxpayer to claim the credit (Treas. Reg. § 1.25A-1(g)). Dependency and the exemption amount are separate issues, however. According to Chief Counsel Advice in 2002 a taxpayer who can be claimed as a dependent could have a zero exemption amount, but still be able to claim the (Hope) credit.[6]

Once dependency is determined, the rest of the qualifications relate to the student. If the student meets the qualifications then the taxpayer qualifies to claim the credit. Some of the qualifications for the AOTC include.

- Student must be pursuing an undergraduate degree or other recognized education credential
- Student must be enrolled at least half time for at least one academic period beginning during the year
- No felony drug conviction on student's record
- Available for first 4 years of post secondary education
- Cannot be claimed more than 4 tax years.

Since the credit is attached to the dependency exemption, if a parent claims the AOTC for a child, the child will not be able to claim it. However, all expenses related to the child are claimed on that credit, whether paid by the student, or parent, or a third party (if paid to the institution). Additional qualifications for the taxpayer include an income threshold and phase-out. Currently the credit is available for taxpayers with a MAGI of less than $90,000 ($180,000 joint returns). MAGI takes into consideration several foreign deductions and exclusions.

Refundable Qualifications

Additional qualifications exist for the refundable portion of the credit. Students age 24 and over qualify for the refundable portion of the credit, as well as parents of children under the age of 24 if they claim the child as a dependent. While many students under the age of 24 do not qualify for the refundable portion of the credit, it is important to review the regulations that apply to each case as there are several exceptions. Filing a joint return or when both parents are deceased are two cases where a student under age 24 could qualify.

---

6   http://www.irs.gov/pub/irs-wd/0236001.pdf

Students that are age 18 and over may also qualify if they provide more than half of their support through earned income, or if they are only attending part-time.

Recent proposals have suggested that the qualifying age be reduced to 21, so a review of current laws may be appropriate. Taxpayers can also use the IRS Interactive Tax Assistant on the IRS website at http://www.irs.gov/uac/Am-I-Eligible-to-Claim-an-Education-Credit%3F to see if they qualify.

Publication 970 provides these qualifications for the refundable part of the credit.

You **do not** qualify for a refund if items 1 (a, b, or c), 2, **and** 3 below apply to you.

1. You were:

   a) Under age 18 at the end of the tax year, **or**

   b) Age 18 at the end of the tax year **and** your earned income (defined below) was less than one-half of your support (defined below), **or**

   c) Over age 18 and under age 24 at the end of the tax year **and** a full-time student (defined below) **and** your earned income (defined below) was less than one-half of your support (defined below).

2. At least one of your parents was alive at the end of the tax year.

3. You are filing a return as single, head of household, qualifying widow(er), or married filing separately.

It is important to notice the ands and ors, and verify any information to the contrary. It may be more useful if the qualifications show who does qualify. Changing some terms and the ands and ors, you may be able to use the following alternate outline.

You DO qualify for a refund if items 1 (a, b, or c), 2, **or** 3 below apply to you.

1. You were:

    a) Age 18 at the end of the tax year **and** your earned income (defined below) was at least one-half of your support (defined below), **or**

    b) Over age 18 and under age 24 at the end of the tax year **and** not a full-time student (defined below), **or**

    c) Over age 18 and under age 24 at the end of the tax year **and** your earned income (defined below) was at least one-half of your support (defined below), **or**

    d) At least age 24.

2. Neither of your parents was alive at the end of the tax year.

3. You are filing a joint return.

Note that the tax code defines those who do not qualify through a series of referrals. See IRC § 25A(i)(5) and references for specific details. The refundable credit is not available to a child to whom IRC § 1(g) (Kiddie tax) applies, which refers to IRC § 152(c)(3). Although IRC § 152(c)(3) includes simply a student under 24, the definition of student in this section is a full-time student as defined in IRC § 152(f)(2)(A). A recent private letter ruling clarifies this restriction.[7]

Fortunately dependency rules may avoid having to make the determination since the credit cannot be claimed if the student doesn't claim his own exemption. Unfortunately, it's possible that neither the taxpayer nor the student can claim the refundable portion of the credit. If the student provides more than half of his own support through unearned income, he cannot be claimed as a dependent, but since the support is not through earned income he might not be able to claim the refundable portion of the credit. Furthermore, since the credit is divided into refundable and nonrefundable, he cannot get the full credit even if tax liability was more than $2,500.

---

7   http://www.irs.gov/pub/irs-wd/201509030.pdf

Flowcharts

The following flowcharts can assist in determining or explaining eligibility.

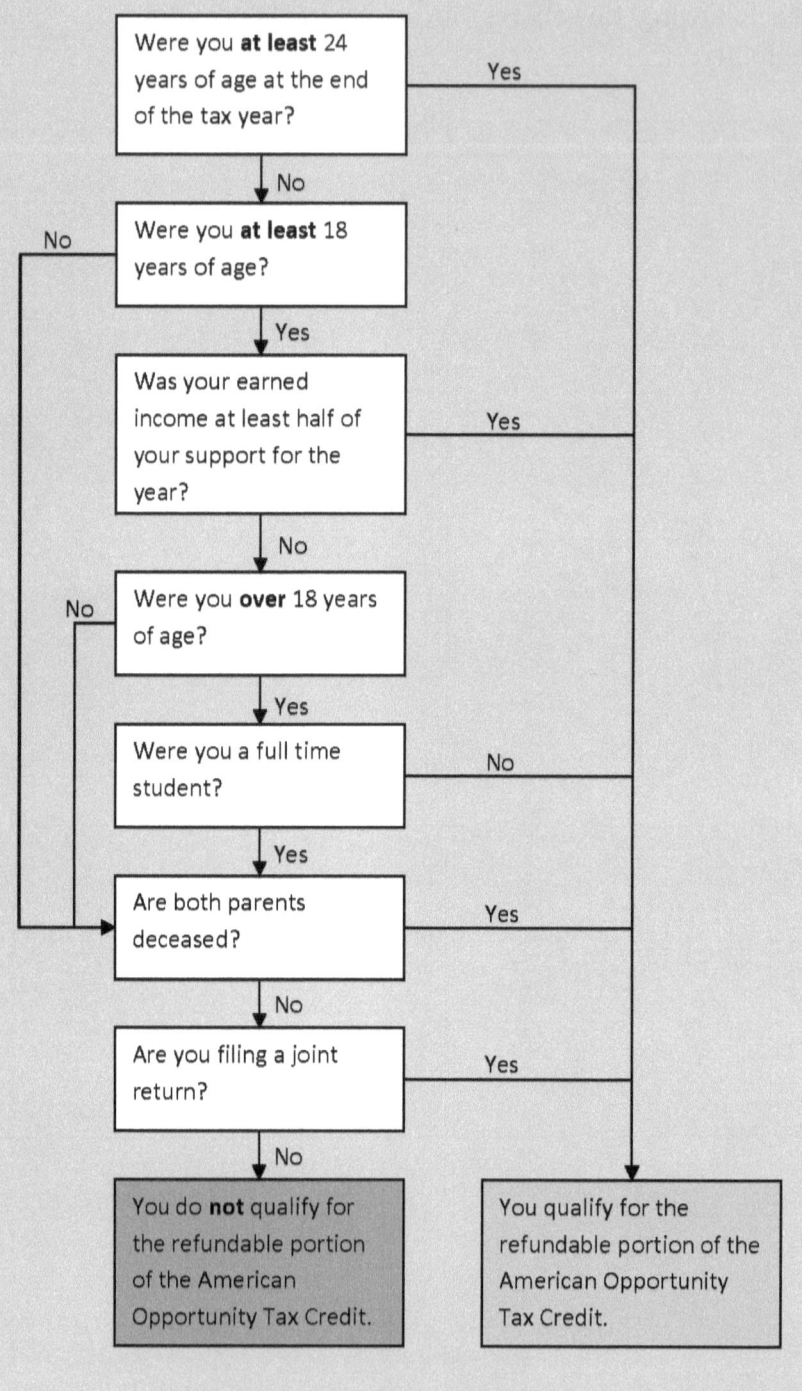

American Opportunity Tax Credit Refundable Credit Test

Were you **at least** 24 years of age at the end of the tax year? — Yes

No ↓

Were you **at least** 18 years of age? — No

Yes ↓

Was your earned income at least half of your support for the year? — Yes

No ↓

Were you **over** 18 years of age? — No

Yes ↓

Were you a full time student? — No

Yes ↓

Are both parents deceased? — Yes

No ↓

Are you filing a joint return? — Yes

No ↓

You do **not** qualify for the refundable portion of the American Opportunity Tax Credit.

You qualify for the refundable portion of the American Opportunity Tax Credit.

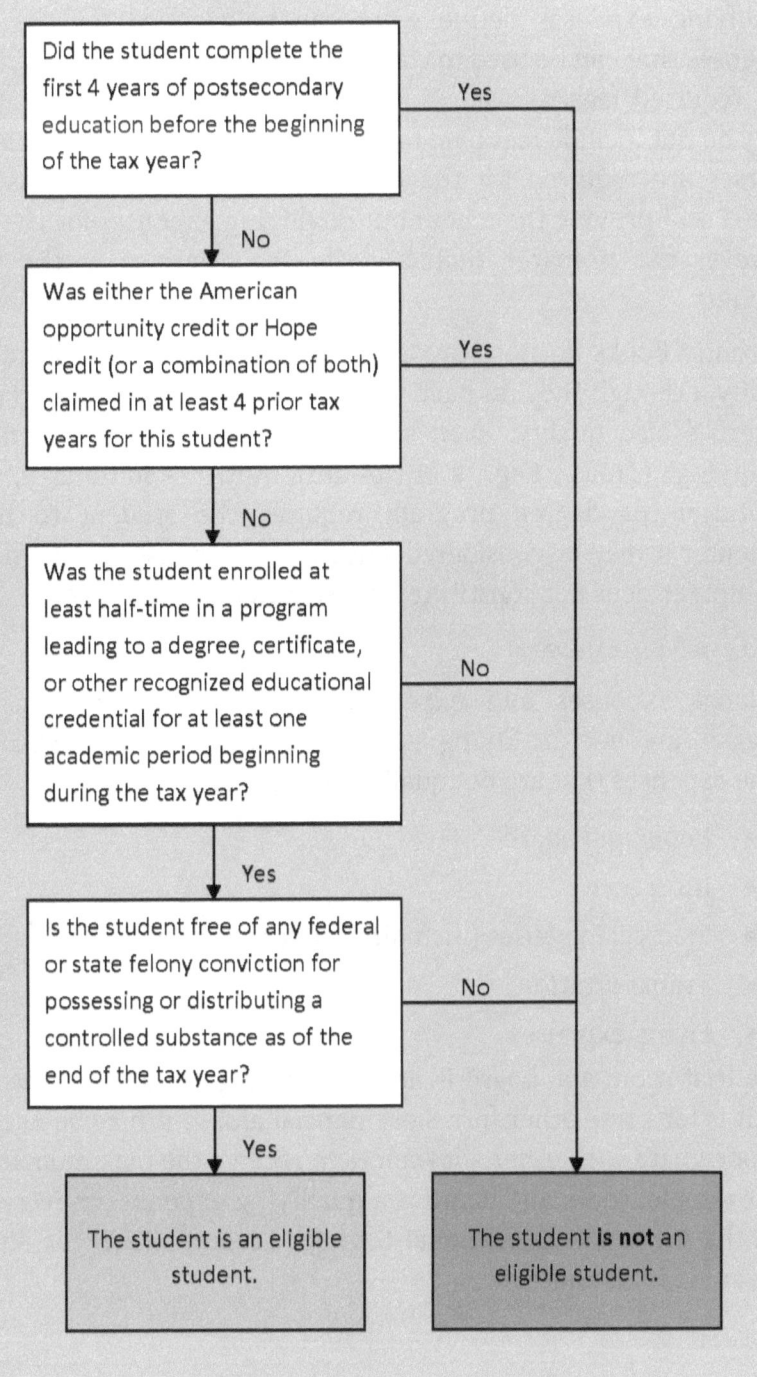

American Opportunity Tax Credit Student Qualifications Test

Did the student complete the first 4 years of postsecondary education before the beginning of the tax year?

Yes →

No ↓

Was either the American opportunity credit or Hope credit (or a combination of both) claimed in at least 4 prior tax years for this student?

Yes →

No ↓

Was the student enrolled at least half-time in a program leading to a degree, certificate, or other recognized educational credential for at least one academic period beginning during the tax year?

No →

Yes ↓

Is the student free of any federal or state felony conviction for possessing or distributing a controlled substance as of the end of the tax year?

No →

Yes ↓

The student is an eligible student.

The student **is not** an eligible student.

Qualifying Expenses

Qualifying expenses define what can be claimed for the AOTC. Expenses that can be used to claim the credits include costs of tuition and required fees, as well as required books and course materials. They do not include fees paid for sports, games, or hobbies unless the courses are required for the degree program. In many cases, the 1098-T will provide the amount of qualifying expenses for the AOTC; however the preparer should verify the accuracy of the 1098-T amounts.

Currently books do not have to be purchased at the institution to qualify although they do have to be required. Other required course materials also qualify. Even some nonacademic expenses may be qualifying (Treas. Reg. § 1.25A-2(d)(2)(iii)). Additionally, if an institution or degree program requires the student to have a computer it may be considered a qualifying expense. Simply needing a computer does not constitute an institutional requirement.

Non Qualifying Expenses

Personal expenses and expenses unrelated to the educational program are not qualifying expenses (Treas. Reg. § 1.25A-2(d)(3)). Some expenses that are not qualifying expenses include

- Room and board
- Insurance
- Medical Expenses (including student health fees)
- Transportation
- Living expenses

Note that room and board is not a qualifying expense for the AOTC, but it is for some other forms of financial aid, so it may be necessary to coordinate with other allowances to receive the maximum benefit. For example, room and board is a qualifying expense for Section 529 and the Coverdell Educational Savings Account (ESA) for students that are at least half-time.

Eligible Educational Institution

Qualifying expenses are limited to tuition and fees paid to an eligible educational institution. IRC § 25A(f)(2) defines the eligible programs with reference to Title IV of the Higher Education Act of 1965. The institution must be an eligible program as defined by 20 USC § 1088(b) and must be eligible to participate in Title IV programs. Title IV programs include various grants and loans authorized by the federal government, such as Pell grants and federally insured student loans. An on-line class in an eligible program does qualify.

Qualifying Payments

In addition to having qualifying expenses, the taxpayer must have made payments for those expenses in tax year. Payments for qualifying expenses include amounts paid by the student, or by the taxpayer, or paid through student loans. Payments can be made by cash or credit. All expenses can be claimed by taxpayers that claim the student as an exemption on their tax return (Treas. Reg. § 1.25A-5(a)).

Payments made by a third party that are in the nature of a gift are also qualifying as paid by the taxpayer. So if a grandparent pays the institution for part of the cost of attending college, the taxpayer can claim the credit using those amounts. The code defines third party expenditures with the phrase, "directly to an eligible educational institution to pay for a student's qualified tuition and related expenses" (Treas. Reg. § 1.25A-5(b)). IRS Publications, however, do not include the restriction that third party payments are made to the institution. Also included in amounts considered paid by the taxpayer are certain scholarships that the taxpayer includes in income. This is discussed in detail later.

The school term for which expenses are paid is also important. Generally payments must be made in the year the term begins. There is one exception. If the payments are made for qualifying expenses for the first three months of the following year, they can be considered as qualifying in the year paid. Payments made in the tax year after the beginning of the school term are not qualified payments (Treas. Reg. § 1.25A-5(e)). For example, if the term begins in December, payments made in the following year do not qualify for that term, even if it ends in the following year. This is more likely to be the possible in a quarter-based school than a semester-based school.

Note: A special rule applies to qualified installment agreements which could delay the recognition of payments for purposes of claiming education credits (Treas. Reg. § 1.25A-5(e)(4)). Tax preparers should review the terms of the agreement to determine when the payments are considered paid and if they qualify as being paid in the tax year.

Payments made through student loans are considered paid when the expenses have been paid by the loan originator.

Lifetime Learning Credit

The LLC is similar to the AOTC in that qualifying expenses are required, but the credit is not refundable. The LLC credit amount is only 20% of expenses. Other differences also exist. Whether you use the LLC or decide to take a deduction may depend on your marginal tax rate as well as MAGI. The credit is phased out for modified MAGI between $52,000 ($104,000 joint), and $62,000 ($124,000 joint).

Qualifications

The LLC does not have as stringent student qualifications. While it must be at an eligible educational institution, it does not require the student to be seeking a degree credential (Treas. Reg. § 1.25A-4(c)). The expenses can be used to pay for expenses as part of a post-secondary degree program or to simply help the student to acquire or improve a job skill. The LLC does not require half-time attendance and isn't limited by a drug felony conviction. Up to $10,000 of expenses can be considered in calculating the credit (IRC § 25A(c)). The taxpayer can take the credit for an unlimited number of years.

Qualifying Expenses

Qualifying expenses for the LLC include costs of tuition and required fees, as well as required books. Although qualified expenses do not include nonacademic fees such as student activity fees, according to IRC § 25A(f)(1)(C)), they are included if they are required as a condition of enrollment (Treas. Reg. § 1.25A-2(d)(2)(iii)). Some academic fees are never included, including transportation expenses such as parking fees (Treas. Reg. § 1.25A(d)(3)).

The inclusion of "course materials" is an AOTC specific allowance (IRC § 25A(i)(3), but there is no clear definition of course materials in the code. According to IRS publications, though, books DO have to be required and purchased at the institution to be qualified expenses for the LLC. Expenses can also be prepaid for the first three months of the following year.

Deductions

Tuition and Fees Deduction

A deduction for educational expenses is also available to taxpayers. The deduction lowers the amount of taxable income. As a deduction the benefit to a particular taxpayer may also be reflected in their marginal tax rate. Generally speaking, if the taxpayer is in a tax bracket higher than 20% (LLC credit amount) the tuition deduction will be the best choice. Because the tuition deduction is a reduction of AGI it could interact with AOTC for another student and any other item linked to the AGI.

The student requirements are similar to the requirements for a credit, although the expense restrictions are similar to the LLC. The code refers to the definition of qualifying expenses provided in IRC § 25A(f), but includes only "qualified tuition and related expenses" (IRC § 222(d)(1)). According to IRS publications, all amounts must be paid to the institution as a condition of enrollment. In other words, if the student has the option of purchasing course materials elsewhere they are not deductible even if purchased from the institution (Publication 970).

Currently, taxpayers can take up to $4,000 deduction for tuition expenses (IRC § 222(b)(3)). Payments for qualifying expenses must be paid by the taxpayer or spouse. Payments made by dependents or third parties do not qualify. The expenses can be for undergraduate or graduate studies and the phase-out begins at $60,000 ($130,000 joint). The deduction is not available to taxpayers with MAGI over $80,000 ($160,000 joint). The AGI modifications do not include the tuition deduction and other adjustments (IRC § 222(b)(2)(C)). Similarly, modifications of AGI for the AOTC don't include adjustments for the tuition deduction.

The rules for LLC and the tuition deduction are different so it will be necessary to determine if the taxpayer qualifies before making that decision. Deciding between this deduction and the LLC will depend on differences in qualifying expenses, payments, treatment of dependent scholarships, and the taxpayer's marginal tax rate. If the taxpayer is in the 25% tax bracket, the deduction is the equivalent of a 25% tax credit on the same amount, although there could be some side effects related to a difference in AGI. The EITC could be affected by excluding tuition expenses from AGI.

Benefit Comparison

The IRS provides a summary comparison of these three benefits at http://www.eitc.irs.gov/Other-Refundable-Credits/educompchart. There are several other benefits that can be used when considering educational expenses and taxation.

Criteria	AOTC	LLC	Tuition and Fees Deduction
Maximum credit or benefit	Up to $2,500 credit per eligible student	Up to $2,000 credit per return	Up to $4,000 taxable income reduction per return
Refundable or nonrefundable	40% of credit	Not refundable	Does not apply

Limit on MAGI* for married filing jointly	$180,000	$128,000	$160,000
Limit on MAGI* for single, head of household, or qualifying widow(er)	$90,000	$64,000	$80,000
Can you file married filing separately?	No		
Dependent status	Cannot claim credit if you are claimed as a dependent on someone else's return		
Must you or your spouse be a U.S. Citizen or Resident Alien?	Yes, unless nonresident alien is treated as resident alien for tax purposes (see Publication 519 for information on nonresident alien status)		
Number of years of post-secondary education available	Only if student hasn't completed 4 years of post secondary education before 2014	All years of post secondary education and for courses to acquire or improve job skills	All years of post secondary education
Number of tax years credit available	4 tax years per eligible student including any years former Hope credit claimed	Unlimited	Unlimited
Type of program required	Student must be pursuing a degree or other recognized education credential	Student does not need to be pursuing a degree or other recognized education credential	Student must be enrolled at eligible educational institution for one or more courses

Number of courses	Student must be enrolled at least half time for at least one academic period beginning in 2014	Available for one or more courses	Available for one or more courses at eligible educational institution
Felony drug conviction	No felony drug convictions as of the end of 2014	Does not apply	Does not apply
Qualified expenses	Tuition, required enrollment fees and course materials needed for course of study	Tuition and fees required for enrollment or attendance	Tuition and fees required for enrollment or attendance
Whom can you claim the benefit for?	You Your spouse Student you claim as a dependent on your return		
Who must pay the qualified expenses?	You or your spouse Student Third party	You or your spouse Student Third party	You or your spouse
Payments for academic periods	Made in 2014 for academic periods beginning in 2014 or the first 3 months of 2015		
Do I need to claim the credit or deduction on a schedule or form?	Yes, Form 8863, Education Credits Form 8863 Instructions	Yes, Form 8863, Education Credits Form 8863 Instructions	Yes, Form 8917, Tuition and Fees Deduction

Business Deduction for Work-Related Education

A related deduction for education expenses required for work can be claimed as an itemized deduction. Although it doesn't require attendance at an eligible institution, there are rules concerning what qualifies as work-related. You can deduct the cost of qualifying work-related education as a business expense if it meets these two tests

- The education is required by your employer or the law to keep your present salary, status or job. The required education must serve a bona fide business purpose of your employer.
- The education maintains or improves skills needed in your present work.

AND

- It is **not** needed to meet the minimum educational requirements of your present trade or business or
- It is **not** a part of a program of study that will qualify you for a new trade or business.

This may be considered a last resort deduction, since the rules are so complex and it requires itemizing deductions. Expenses for books, supplies, certain transportation, travel, and other necessary expenses can be included.

The deduction must be claimed on Schedule A of an individual return for employees or on a business schedule (Schedule C or Schedule F) for a self-employed person. On Schedule A, expenses are subject to the 2% floor. Reimbursements must be treated according to "accountable plan" rules.

Employer-Provided Educational Assistance

Another benefit is Employer-Provided Educational Assistance. When qualifying benefits are provided to employees, the value of the benefits may not be taxable. Education generally includes any form of instruction or training that improves or develops your capabilities. The payments do not have to be for work-related courses or courses that are part of a degree program. The benefit is limited to $5,250 and is excluded from taxable wages on a W-2. Excess amounts are taxable.

Employer-Provided Educational Assistance is discussed in more detail under Other Educational Incentives later.

No Double Benefit

One of the most important concepts in tax law is "no double benefit." If you claim one benefit, you are generally restricted from claiming a related benefit. This is particularly true regarding educational incentives. You can't claim AOTC and LLC for the same student, nor can you take the tuition deduction for the same student. Similarly, scholarships can't be considered tax-free if the qualifying expenses paid by a scholarship are used to claim a tax credit or deduction.

Even though taxpayers can combine AOTC or LLC with some other tax benefits on a tax return, the same expenses can't be used for more than one benefit. For example, while Section 529, Coverdell Savings Account, and some other tax benefits are generally tax-free, they are not tax-free if used to pay qualifying expenses used to claim an education credit. When multiple tax benefits are involved, understanding how to coordinate the various benefits can assist in maximizing the potential tax breaks.

General Scholarship Treatment

For both the AOTC and LLC, scholarships are often treated as tax-free when applied to qualified expenses, in which case the qualified expenses are reduced by that amount. The tax code defines the term qualified scholarship as any amount used for qualifying expenses refers to both scholarships and grants (IRC § 117(b)(1)). When scholarships are not considered qualified, or tax-free, they are included in the taxpayer's gross income. Similarly, scholarships in excess of qualified expenses are taxable, although some expenses may be qualified tax-free by other plans.

Scholarships (or fellowships) that are paid for services rendered to the institution are not tax-free scholarships and should always be included in income. This might include scholarships that require student teaching or research assistance and would be reported to the taxpayer on a W-2. Some exceptions to this exclusion include the National Health Service Corps Scholarship, the Armed Forces Health Professions Scholarship (IRC § 117(c)), and Qualified Tuition Reduction (IRC § 117(d)).

While scholarships generally offset expenses, the regulations do allow taxpayers to treat some scholarships differently in order to increase their qualifying expenses. That is one of the primary reasons for this text and it is covered in the next section.

Regulations

The tax code in Internal Revenue Code Section 25A outlines the legal requirements (as passed by Congress) for education credits, but there are separate regulations that the IRS has released that define how they will treat education credits and qualifications. The regulations explain how taxpayers should report items for education credits. Treasury regulations answer questions that taxpayers may have concerning the law, and very often they include examples of treatment.

For example, IRC § 25A defines the Hope and Lifetime Learning Credits. IRC § 25A(i) amends that section to include the American Opportunity Tax Credit. Treas. Reg. § 1.25A-1 through Treas. Reg. § 1.25A-5 are the regulations that cover the law in IRC § 25A. In most cases, taxpayers can rely on treasury regulations in reporting their taxes. One of the regulations, Treas. Reg. § 1.25A-5 enhances/clarifies the options taxpayers have when claiming education credits, allowing them to coordinate their benefits to achieve the greatest advantage.

The regulations do provide examples and explanations that can be useful for tax preparers. However, the Treasury Directive (TD 9034) that contained the original regulations can also be useful in explaining other characteristics of the regulations, and answering comments and questions about the regulations.

Initial Regulations

The first four regulations cover the basic requirements for IRC § 25A by describing requirements and calculation of the credits (Treas. Reg. § 1.25A-1), definitions (Treas. Reg. § 1.25A-2), specific requirements for the Hope Credit (Treas. Reg. § 1.25A-3), and specific requirements for the Lifetime Learning Credit (Treas. Reg. § 1.25A-4). These are reflected in the description of the credits above. The last regulation related to IRC § 25A provides guidelines for coordinating scholarships and the expenses used to qualify for the credit.

Coordinating Scholarships to Maximize Credits

Entitled "Special rules relating to characterization and timing of payments," Treas. Reg. § 1.25A-5 gives the procedure for calculating expenses for the credit and outlines the rules for calculating the credit and in particular where scholarships and grants are involved.

In general, education credits are available for amounts that the taxpayer pays and scholarships are tax-free to the degree they are used for qualifying expenses. However, it may be possible to qualify for or increase the amount of both the AOTC and the LLC by including some scholarships and grants in income. This is largely dependent on the type of scholarship or grant.

IRC § 117 defines qualified scholarships as **any amount** of a scholarship used for qualified expenses and requires the qualified expenses for the credit to be reduced to reflect that tax-free nature. However some scholarships can be treated as taxable or non-taxable based on the terms of the scholarship as outlined in Regulation 1.25A-5(c)(3)[8]. The regulation also includes multiple examples illustrating the potential effects of considering scholarship taxable income. For tax purposes grants follow the same logic as scholarships and the IRS has recently focused on Pell grants in making this treatment more familiar.

Three Types of Scholarships

The tax code only describes taxable and qualified (or tax-free) scholarships, and qualified scholarships only describe amounts of a scholarship that are used to pay qualified expenses. In order to better understand the types of scholarships in regards to tax treatment, I define scholarships here as 1) exclusive, 2) taxable, or 3) elective. Briefly, exclusive scholarships cover only qualified expenses, taxable scholarships cover non-qualified expenses, and elective scholarships may be used to cover qualified or non-qualified expenses.[9] Although not defined as such in the code, the three types are covered in IRC §

---

8   http://www.law.cornell.edu/cfr/text/26/1.25A-5. Accessed 11/6/2014.

9   Other discussions have used the terms restricted and unrestricted in comparing exclusive and elective scholarships.

117(b)(1) and Treas. Reg. § 1.25A(c)(3).

Exclusive Scholarships

Exclusive scholarships are those scholarships, by the terms of scholarship, which must be used to pay qualified expenses. The full amount of the scholarships must reduce the amount of qualified expenses. Because the scholarship must be used for qualified expenses, no amount should be refunded. In some cases scholarships terms determine the amount of the scholarship based on the *amount* of qualified expenses, but that may not indicate that the funds must be used for those expenses. The Louisiana TOPS case, later, describes such a scenario. Still, the conservative treatment is to consider scholarships exclusive until determined otherwise.

Taxable Scholarships

A scholarship that **must be used** exclusively for **other than** qualified expenses is taxable. It is reported on line 7 as scholarship income with other taxable scholarships. Room and board is not a qualifying expense, so scholarships that cover only that is normally taxable. Scholarships in excess of qualifying expenses are also treated as taxable scholarships. As you will see next, some scholarships can be **treated** as taxable scholarships.

A scholarship that pays students for services they must perform, such as teaching or research, are generally taxable and reported as earned income on a W-2. They should not enter into the calculation of education credits.

Elective Scholarships

The third type of scholarship is the elective scholarship. The elective nature of these scholarships is what enables us to re-allocate scholarship amounts effectively increasing qualified expenses to achieve the highest credit amount.

The term *elective* is not described in the code as such but the concept is taken from Treas. Reg. § 1.25A-5(c)(3) where scholarship amounts can be treated as either taxable or tax-free. The concept is also published in IRS Publication 970. The phrase that separates exclusive from elective in this context is "used for other than qualified expenses." If a scholarship **may** or **must** be used for other than qualified expenses you can elect to include it in income, or treat it as tax-free and offset qualified expenses. When treated as income, the amount of qualified expenses is not reduced and the taxpayer may qualify for a higher education credit.

Pell Grants

Scholarships that are available for elective treatment include Pell grants. In fact, determining if other scholarships are elective will often not be necessary. Pell grants may often be $4000 or more of the aid received by the student, the maximum amount considered in calculating the AOTC. The LLC expense limit is $10,000. Most other federal aid, as well as Coverdell Educational Savings Accounts and Section 529 accounts can also be treated as elective scholarships (IRC § 530(d)(2)(C)).

Measured Scholarships

Although there is no regulation that addresses scholarships that are "measured by" the amount of tuition, as opposed to "used for" tuition, IRS rulings do support the elective nature of such scholarships. While that may seem to be simply semantics, a change in the wording was the defining characteristic that allowed scholarship inclusion in the Louisiana TOPS program. Just because a scholarship is based on the costs of tuition does not mean it is limited to tuition costs. In an IRS private letter ruling (PLR) related to the Louisiana Tuition Opportunity Program for Students (TOPS) program in Louisiana, it was determined that the TOPS awards could be applied to Section 25A and 117 in determining tax treatment. [10]

In 1999 the Louisiana legislature went from a system that required a TOPS award to be used for tuition to a system that measures the amount of the award by the amount of tuition. In that program the amount of the scholarship is limited to the amount of tuition, and the IRS has determined that this scholarship qualifies to be included in

---

10 www.irs.gov/pub/irs-wd/0137006.pdf (PLR 200137006)

income to increase QE for education credits.

Although PLRs cannot be used as precedent, the logic can be used to make the case for similar scenarios. The TOPS ruling confirms that (then proposed) Treas. Reg. § 1.25A-5(c)(3) allows this grant to be considered a "qualified scholarship excludable from income under section 117" unless:

> (i) The grant is reported as income on the taxpayer's federal income tax return, or

> (ii) The grant must be applied, by its terms, to expenses other than qualified tuition and related expenses within the meaning of section 117(b)(2), such as room and board."

Following the ruling, the Louisiana Law Review published an article encouraging recipients of the TOPS grant to consider using Treasury Reg. 1.25A-5 to amend their returns to claim prior year education credits.[11]

Following are excerpts from the PLR

> 4. Federal tax consequences of the Louisiana TOPS Award under §§ 25A and 117.

> As noted earlier, prior to being amended in 1999, Louisiana law required that awards made to students under the TOPS program be spent on tuition. As such, the amount of any award was excludable from gross income under § 117 and reduced the amount of qualified expenses eligible for the education tax credit. However, in 1999, the Louisiana legislature amended the TOPS statute for the express purpose of qualifying a student or his parent or guardian for the § 25A credit. The legislature amended the TOPS statute to –

> (1) provide that TOPS awards are in an amount equal to tuition (rather than being for tuition);

> (2) cause the administering agency to direct the institution that whenever the TOPS award is paid on behalf of the student and the

---

11   http://digitalcommons.law.lsu.edu/cgi/viewcontent.cgi?
     article=5806&context=lalrev

student's tuition is paid from a source other than the TOPS award, the award is to be applied by the educational institution toward payment of those "costs of attendance" other than tuition; and

(3) permit a student to elect to defer receipt of a TOPS award and to spend the amount received on costs of attendance other than tuition and provide that the amount of the award will be reduced if a § 25A credit is claimed.

..

We view these statutory provisions as terms of the grant and discuss below the effect the Service should give these terms in applying §§ 25A and 117 to award recipients.

..

Under the terms of the grant as we construe them, therefore, the Service should give effect to Louisiana's changes under (1), above, which permit the award to be used for either qualifying or non-qualifying expenses. Under this interpretation, the exclusion of the grant is determined by the tax reporting of the grantee.

The terms of the Texas Grant now contains similar wording and may be considered elective in the same manner as the TOPS. As more taxpayers take advantage of Regulation 1.25A-5(c)(3), the IRS may issue other regulations clarifying what constitutes elective scholarships.

On the other hand, the Texas Hazlewood Exemption for Texas veterans would not be considered elective because of its strict regulation that amounts are for tuition and required fees, and because it is an exemption rather than an amount provided to the taxpayer.

Other Elective Scholarships

If it's necessary to consider the elective nature of other scholarships research will be required, but that research outlay can be used on multiple returns. A practitioner that researches area scholarships in advance can quickly answer questions about the elective nature of particular scholarships. A repository of information related to these scholarships will be invaluable during tax season. Finding out if scholarships can be taxable can be a formidable task, however. The following section on Scholarship Research may help in that endeavor.

Dual Requirements

In some cases, scholarships may be required to be used for a combination of qualifying and non-qualifying expenses, for example, only tuition and room and board. These scholarships would be partially exclusive and partially elective. If that is the case, the amount must be allocated between the two amounts. For example, if a $6,000 scholarship must be used for tuition and room and board, and room and board is $5,000, no more than than amount can be allocated to room and board. At least $1,000 must be allocated to tuition. One of the IRS scenarios in Treas. Reg. § 1.25A-5 explains the treatment of such scholarships and it is discussed later when illustrating the use of the AOTC worksheet.

Lifetime Learning Credit

Although the focus has been on the AOTC, elective scholarships can be treated the same way in calculating the LLC. There are differences in what constitutes qualifying expenses, however. The most notable exception is that books must have been purchased from the institution and may already be included on the 1098-T. The LLC would apply, for example, if the student has already received his 4-year degree before the beginning of the tax year, or was not attending at least half-time. The LLC is not refundable so the benefit is limited to the amount of tax owed, but scholarship inclusion is allowed for the LLC also.

Scholarship Research

One of the most challenging aspects of preparing tax returns for clients claiming education credits which include scholarships in income may be determining what scholarships are elective. It's not a difficult task for most federal grants, but it can be particularly challenging for locally funded scholarships. Following are examples of scholarships that I have determined to be elective, from federal to state and local. Rather than rely on calls and letters to local colleges, I did most of the research on the Internet.

All of the circumstances should be weighed when determining if a scholarship, grant, or other source is evaluated for possible treatment as an elective scholarship suitable for maximizing the education credits. However, some key words to look for are "room and board", "living expenses", "housing", and "excess refunded". While "excess refunded" is not a key term for IRS rules, it is a good indicator. It is important that a review of the terms do not require that certain costs be paid for with the scholarships.

Federal Grants

Federal grants are a common source of financial aid. Most federal aid, including the Pell Grants, are need-based, and since the term "need" includes food and a place to stay, you might conclude that they may be used for other than qualified expenses. You don't have to wrangle with that. The federal student aid website provides this Q&A.

Q6. What costs does a Federal Pell Grant cover?

A6. Federal Pell Grants are available if you are taking classes as part of a program that leads to an undergraduate degree or certificate. Federal student aid, including Pell Grants, can be used to cover a variety of costs, generally including

Tuition and fees normally assessed;

Books, supplies, transportation, and miscellaneous personal expenses;

Living expenses such as room and board; and

An allowance for costs expected to be incurred for dependent care for a student with dependents.[12]

The IRS and the Treasury Department have specifically promoted the inclusion of Pell grants in income to qualify for education credits.

State Scholarships

TSBPA

The Texas State Board of Public Accountability (TSBPA) Fifth-Year Accounting Student Scholarship was one that has applied to me in the past and I found this line on the TSBPA website that describes the uses for the award:

The award may be used at a participating college or university in Texas that is recognized by the Board. The award may be used for tuition, fees, books, supplies, and living expenses incurred by the student in connection with the student's fifth year of an accounting program.[13]

Although this scholarship covers expenses for a five-year degree, it doesn't change the requirements for the AOTC. However, if the student has not "earned" a bachelor's degree **before** the **beginning** of the tax year he may still meet the requirements for AOTC even though he is taking graduate level classes.

TEXAS Grant

The TEXAS Grant terms are similar to the terms of the Louisiana TOPS program that measures the amount of the grant by the amount of the tuition and fees. As such, it would likely be considered eligible for the same treatment. The promotional website contains the following

The maximum award amount (including state and institutional

---

12   http://federalstudentaid.ed.gov/opportunity/questions.html,   Accessed 3/25/2014.

13   http://www.tsbpa.state.tx.us/scholarship/awards-uses-for-the-award.html, Accessed 3/25/2014.

funds) is equal to the student's tuition and required fees.

That wording and the lack of related restrictions in the supporting regulation suggests that you can include it in income in order to increase education credits.

Local Research Examples

There are also official representations of the terms of several popular scholarships in Tyler institutions' websites.

UT Tyler

In most of the endowed UT Tyler scholarships, the first item describing the requirements is "Award may be used for the payment of tuition, fees, books and supplies at UT Tyler only." and then there is an addition that "Any remaining funds will be disbursed on the published financial aid disbursement date." If you apply logic, it seems to allow you to use remaining funds for personal expenses, and thus it may be used for other than qualified expenses. Fortunately, you don't have to twist any words here either. The UT Tyler Scholarship FAQ page confirms:

> Q: Will scholarship awards apply to tuition, fees, books, supplies, and housing?
>
> A: Yes, up to the value of the award.
>
> Q: If I have monies left over on my account after everything is paid, will I get those monies?
>
> A: Yes... Remaining funds will be refunded....[14]

Since the scholarship can be used for housing, it would clearly fit the mold for elective treatment. I suspect such elective scholarships are more common today because institutions don't want to keep track of whether you use the resources for qualified expenses. Everything is grouped together in the student's account, tuition and fees are paid, and the excess is refunded. However, it is best to find something that indicates a scholarship is elective.

---

14 http://www.uttyler.edu/scholarships/faq.php, Accessed 3/25/2014.

Faulconer Scholarship

Another local scholarship available at Tyler Junior College is the Faulconer Scholarship. Faulconer Scholarships are awarded to African-American or Hispanic high school students who are graduating seniors living within the Tyler Junior College Tax District. The home page for the scholarship describes the qualifications and answers questions concerning the use of the scholarship. While the scholarship amounts may change depending on other aid the use of the funds meets the description of an elective scholarship.

> *What can the scholarship be used for?*
>
> *Your scholarship funds should be used to pay any regular educational fees at college, such as books, tuition, fees, supplies or meal tickets, room and board if needed. If, at the end of the year, you have not spent all of your scholarship funds, you may receive a refund from your college account. Unless you spend the refunded money toward your college expense, you may be subject to income tax on the balance refunded to you.[15]*

Aid Designed for Scholarship Inclusion

While tax professionals should not assume all scholarships can be treated as elective, it appears that institutions and agencies are designing financial aid in order to avoid that aid being a barrier to claiming education credits. In some cases, managing the scholarships for qualifying expenses may just be too much trouble for the institutions. Many scholarships allow a refund of amounts not used. In other cases, guidelines are being changed to actually allow students to maximize the education credits. The TOPS case is one such instance, and the Texas Grant is also structured to allow scholarship inclusion using the same type of wording.

Given the tax law knowledge and research information, the next steps involved in claiming an education credit would include

- Document Preparation – accessing records of expenses and payments

---

15 http://faulconerscholars.org/?page_id=83

- Student Account Tabulation – totaling the expenses and payments
- Tax Credit Calculation – calculating the maximum credit

Document Preparation

Claiming an education credit begins with obtaining the necessary information. Accessing and organizing information on qualifying expenses and payments is essential to preparing accurate returns. While a taxpayer may provide a 1098-T, it is better if the information can be verified with information from the institution. Not only are they needed to calculate the credit, document preparation is also important because the information forms the basis for documentation should the IRS request it. If scholarships are involved, the institutional records are needed to identify elective scholarships and resources.

The biggest issue related to claiming education credits may be acquiring the necessary records. Very often the taxpayer will not provide anything but the 1098-T, and in many cases they do not even receive one of them. It is possible to ask them to get the information from the college but it may be more practical to guide them in accessing the records or access them yourself.

Practitioners can have the client log into the account or provide the login information and then access, copy, and format the data themselves. That would alleviate some of the taxpayer's frustration and possibly avoid time-consuming errors. Generally, I ask the taxpayers to log in to their account on-site and I then copy the information to a spreadsheet where I can properly evaluate the expenses. Although most institutions provide online access to student financial records, some are not easily transferred. The local university, for example, can show the amounts paid on the website but the software doesn't support printing a complete list of transactions unless they are visible on screen.

The most difficult situations are where the scholarships cover expenses and the institution does not provide students with the 1098-T. This simple guide can assist in gathering the necessary information to determine if the taxpayer qualifies for an education credit. This includes a description of the 1098-T first and later includes instructions for getting educational expense information from two of the local colleges, UT Tyler and Tyler Junior College. Practitioners not in the Tyler area may want to create their own guide for accessing account information from colleges and universities in that area. Instructions for accessing prior year tax return information for amending returns is also provided later.

1098-T

Not Always Provided

The first item that should be reviewed and added to the documentation for education credits is a copy of the 1098-T, if the institution provided one. Institutions are not required to release a 1098-T if financial aid covers all of the expenses (Treas. Reg. § 1.6050S-1(a)(2)(iii)). If that is the case, don't waste time waiting for one to come in the mail. I am told that the local university, UT Tyler, now provides 1098-Ts to all students, while Tyler Junior College does still limit them to students with expenses greater than scholarships and grants.

Although the following statement appears on the most current TJC website, it is not necessarily true. Remember that students have the option of including some scholarships in income in order to qualify for tax credits.

> It's tax time! 1098-T forms have been mailed to students who qualify for the tuition tax credit.
>
> How do I know if I qualified for the tax credit and if I am eligible to receive this form?
>
> Did you have financial aid or scholarships?
>
> Did you receive a refund of financial aid (excluding student loans)?
>
> If you answered yes to both of the above questions, more than likely you did not qualify to receive the tax form as you were not out of pocket to pay for your tuition and fees.

Please check online at www.1098-T.com to see if there is a form available for you. If nothing comes up, then you more than likely did not qualify and will not be receiving the form. For more information on whether or not you qualify for the tax credit, please see the website.

It is the practice and policy of Tyler Junior College to only mail forms to students who qualify to claim the tax credit when filing their income tax.

Unfortunately similar advice can be found on many other college websites.

Not Required (until 2016)

The fact that a student doesn't receive a 1098-T is confusing to taxpayers. Taxpayers should understand that not receiving a 1098-T may not limit their ability to claim a credit. Many taxpayers may have been missing out on the AOTC for this reason alone. The requirement to have a 1098-T is a new law that does not go into effect until the 2016 tax year.

Not Enough Information

Even if you have the 1098-T, in many cases the 1098-T doesn't provide enough information. The IRS requires some institutions to provide students with a 1098-T showing expenses and aid received, and Form 8863 provides areas to enter the amounts but IRS instructions include the admonition to verify the accuracy of 1098-T amounts. That admonition should be heeded because 1098-T amounts may often be inaccurate. Some reasons may include

- **Expenses and scholarships are mismatched on the 1098-T.** All scholarships and grants are reported on the 1098-T whether for qualified or non-qualified expenses, but only qualified expenses are reported on the 1098-T.

- **The reported amounts are often misaligned chronologically.** The institution has the option of reporting amounts paid or amounts billed. Very often the amounts shown as billed in the current year are for a term in the following tax year, while scholarships are not being provided until that following year.

- **Not all qualified expenses appear on a 1098-T.** In the case of the AOTC, students could incur qualified expenses, such as books, that are not reported on a 1098-T.

- **Some scholarships and grants can be included in income.** Taxpayers may be able to include certain scholarships and grants in income to increase the education credit.

- **Institutional reporting options.** The institution has options for reporting billed or paid amounts, and timing of payments based on boxes checked.

It's true that the 1098-T can sometimes provide enough information to calculate the credit, but those situations are limited. The most informative 1098-T is one in which qualifying expenses are reported in box 1 and there is no check in box 7. If there is an amount given for scholarships taxpayers can take the difference and find either net qualifying expenses (if expenses are greater than scholarships) or excess scholarships. That assumes the amounts reported are correct for the credit being claimed. This doesn't, however, maximize the credit for the taxpayer if some of the scholarships are Pell grants or similar scholarships.

Boxes

Potentially confusing to both taxpayer and preparer are the various ways in which amounts can be reported on a 1098-T. The key items on a 1098-T are

Box 1 – Payments received for qualified tuition and related expenses

Box 2 – Amounts billed for qualified tuition and related expenses

Box 5 – Scholarships or grants

Box 7 – Indicates expenses billed for January – March of the following year

Box 8 – Indicates at least half-time student

Box 9 – Indicates a graduate student

The two most commonly reported amounts on a 1098-T are the expenses in Box 1 or Box 2, and the scholarships and grants reported in Box 5. If those are the only items on the 1098-T then the taxpayer can generally calculate the credit from that and information about the nature of the scholarships.

If box 2 is used instead of box 1, you need to verify that billed amounts were actually paid and if all amounts paid were included in the amount billed.

Amounts Include Following Year

The most challenging forms are those with a check in Box 7, since that indicates some items billed are for the following year. Often institutions bill students in November or December for the spring semester. If scholarships and grants are involved these amounts may likely not be paid in the tax year.

Also, if box 7 is checked in the current year it is likely that the prior year 1098-T included amounts billed in that year (not the tax year) but which are paid in the current tax year. So, box 2 amounts billed may not include all amounts paid in the tax year. The preparer or client should review the student's financial account records for the correct amounts.

Advanced Payments

If amounts billed for the following year are actually paid, then the taxpayer can get a credit for that amount. For qualified expenses on record in December, but for the school term beginning in January of the following year, the payments will be qualified in the year paid. Note, however, that amounts paid in a prior year can only be claimed in that prior year, in line with Treas. Reg. § 1.25A-5(e)(2), and if the payment is for expenses in the first three months of the following year. Current payments for prior year expenses do not qualify.

Qualified Expenses for What?

Even when a 1098-T includes what appears to be the correct amount of qualifying expenses paid, it would be wise to also evaluate that from the actual student expenses. The instructions for preparing a 1098-T are not specific when identifying qualifying expenses and they differ depending on whether the benefit is AOTC, LLC, or a tuition deduction. The institution's classification of qualifying expenses may also vary.

Graduate Student

A check in Box 9 (graduate student) does not necessarily disqualify a student from receiving the AOTC. One of the requirements of AOTC is that the student did not earn a bachelor's degree, but that test is made based on the beginning of the tax year, not the end of the tax year. If a student graduated in May, all expenses for the year qualify for the AOTC.

Adjustments and Corrections

If Box 4 or Box 6 has an amount provided then the taxpayer may need to file an amended return for the prior year. As in other circumstances, whether the taxpayer must amend the return will depend on whether they received a tax benefit (directly or indirectly) for the prior year. If the amendment does not change the tax due, generally no amendment is required.

Box 3 indicates that the method of reporting has changed in the current year. If the student had expenses in the prior year it will be necessary to evaluate that.

Box 10 should also be considered since any reimbursements will reduce the amount of qualifying expenses.

The 1098-T in 2015

As part of the push to educate taxpayers about education credit regulations, there is a change in the 2015 version of the 1098-T. On the instructions on the back of the 2015 1098-T the IRS has provided this tip.

> ...
>
> **Box 5.** Shows the total of all scholarships or grants administered and processed by the eligible educational institution. The amount of scholarships or grants for the calendar year (including those not reported by the institution) may reduce the amount of the education credit you claim for the year.
>
> **TIP.** You may be able to increase the combined value of an education credit and certain educational assistance (including Pell Grants) if the student includes some or all of the educational assistance in income in the year it is received. For details, see Pub. 970.
>
> ...

Even with that change many students will not see that option if the institutions do not have to issue them a 1098-T.

Accessing the 1098-T

Institutions generally mail 1098-T by the end of January of the tax year. In some cases, the form, or a link to it, may be provided through e-mail. If the student doesn't receive a 1098-T they may be able to download one from the institution's website.

In some cases, the institution lets a third-party service handle the availability of 1098-Ts on-line. A key provider for local colleges is at

www.1098t.com

Once you log in you may be shown a page

FORM 1098-T ELECTRONIC DELIVERY AUTHORIZATION

Students don't have to authorize electronic delivery. By authorizing electronic delivery, they will have future forms e-mailed to you instead of receiving paper forms in the mail. Instead, click on the Student Information in the left side panel, and select the year and school, and click "View My 1098-T Tax Form." This will show a PDF download that you can save.

Whether or not taxpayers have a 1098-T it is advisable to get the student's account information to clarify and verify the amounts. The student account will also typically show the name of the scholarship or grant and that can assist in determining if it is an elective scholarship or not.

Following are the procedures for accessing student account information from two of the local schools. Practitioners outside of this area may wish to document the procedures for colleges in their area.

UT Tyler

The myUTTyler website provides UT Tyler students with access to their accounts. Unfortunately, the site does not make it easy to download information on qualifying expenses. Although you can display detailed information, their system currently doesn't support printing that information. Instead, the system will only print the visible screen. Following is one way to get the information that you need from their website if you do not have that information elsewhere. By copying the data from the page into a spreadsheet, it is easier to categorize and total relevant amounts for the calculations. The following was done using the Firefox browser.

Login

Go to your browser and enter

my.uttyler.edu

This will redirect to something that starts with https://sis-portal-prod.uttyler.edu/psp/ and prompts the user to log in.

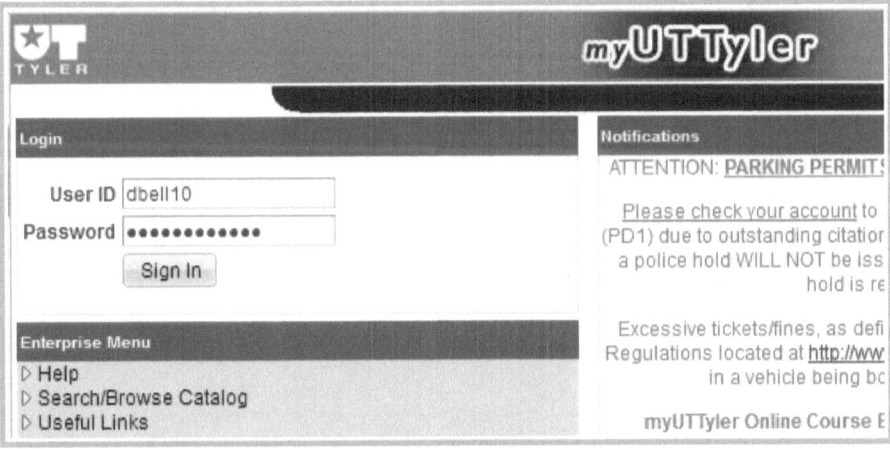

my UTTyler Login

Enter the student's User ID and password and click Sign In. The UserID is normally the part of their patriots email address before the @ sign. Once you are logged in, you will see several items in the left menu

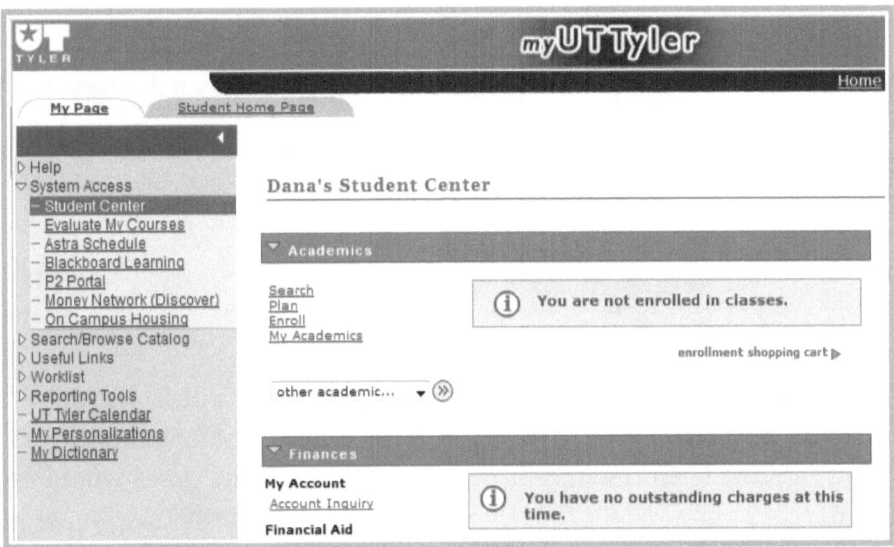

my UTTyler

Click on Student Access, then on Student Center, and under Finances, click Account Inquiry

Education Tax Credits

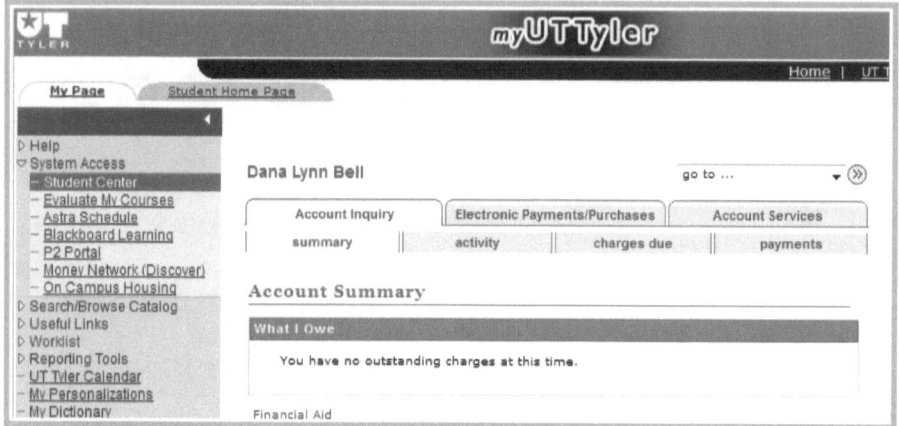

Account Inquiry

The display will then show several tabs at the top with Account Summary as the initial section shown. Click on the Activity sub-tab to select the transactions you will need.

Inquiry

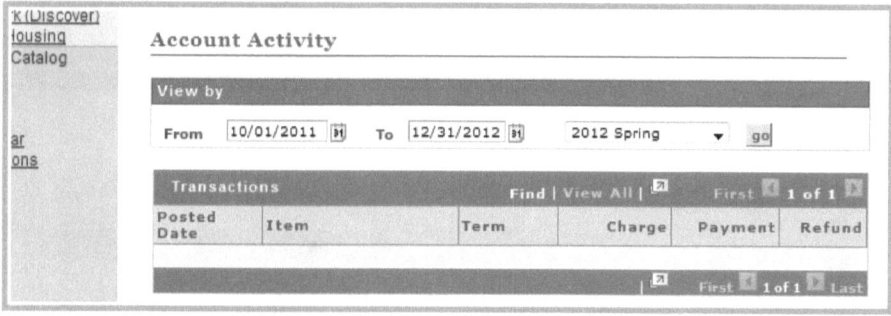

Account Activity

Under the subhead View by, select the dates you want to include in your inquiry. Ideally, enter the date three months before the start of the year, and then the end of the year. For 2014, the dates would be 10/01/2013 and 12/31/2014. Starting in the previous year is necessary because the University enters charges for Spring 2014 at the end of 2013.

Then select the term to report on, and press Go

Term Inquiry

Initially the display will show only 10 lines at a time. Click on 'View All' in the table header to show all transactions (up to 100) for the term. If more than 100 items, you will have to display and process each 100 until complete.

Term Inquiry – All Items

What you do now will depend on what the tax preparer can work with. I haven't been able to print the complete list, so I copy and paste the information from the browser to Excel first.

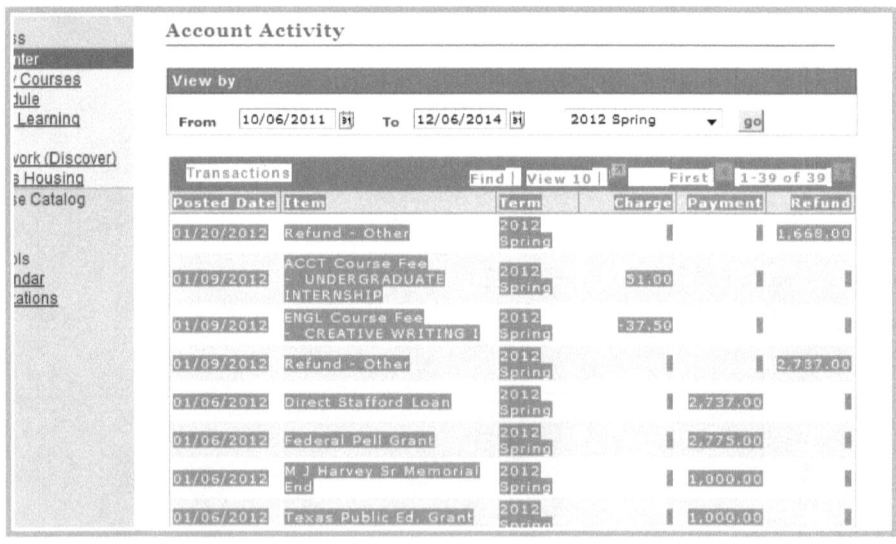

Term Inquiry – Select Items

In order to copy/paste select the information on the page beginning to the left of Transactions head, mark all items in the table. Selecting is done by clicking, holding, and dragging to highlight the information you want. Right-click and select Copy.

Open Excel, select a cell, right-click and select paste. It will not look pretty at first but it can be fixed with a couple of steps.

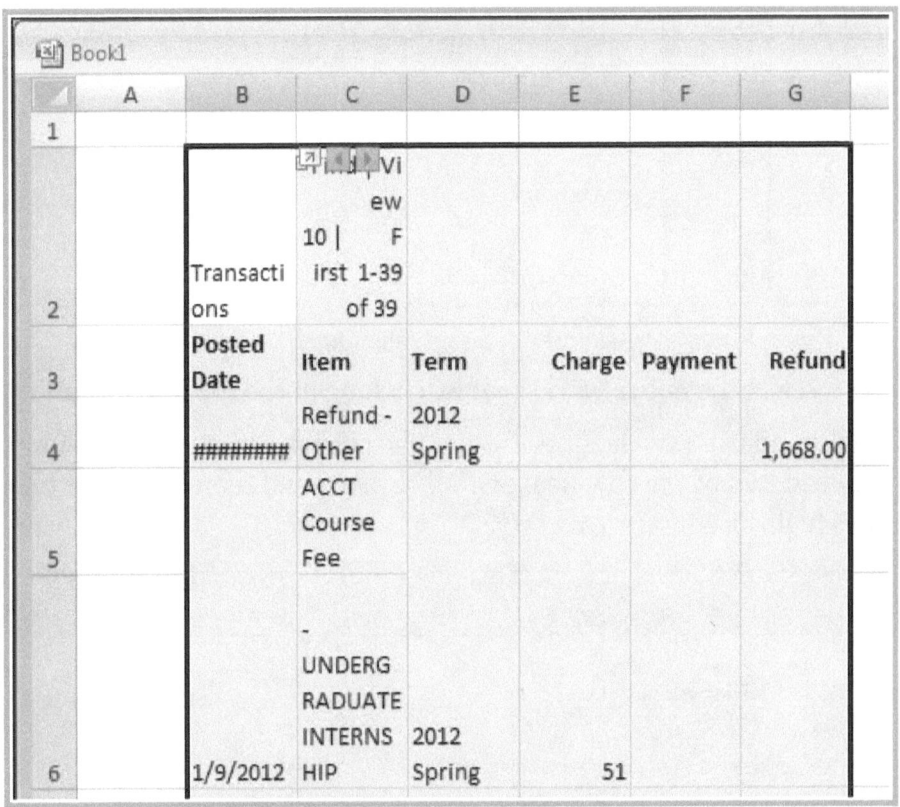

Excel – Paste Items

You may wish to repeat the copy/paste operation for each term before formatting the spreadsheet.

After you have copied the information into the spreadsheet you will need to reposition the columns and format for calculation.

The first step is to adjust the column widths to show all information. Click between the column headers and drag to widen the column to show the information without breaking words and obliterating the dates.

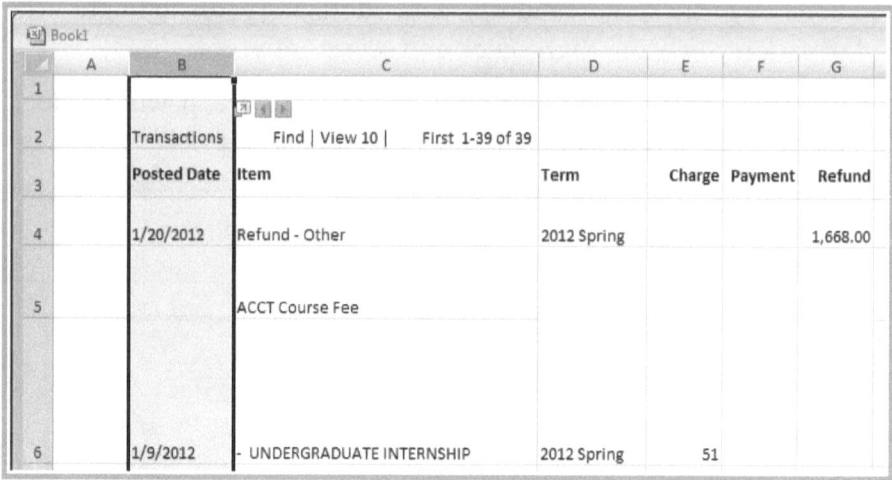

Excel – Column Adjustment

Next, select the entire worksheet by clicking in the top left corner.

Finally, adjust row heights by double clicking in the left column between two of the row headers. All rows should then by one or two lines high.

	A	B	C	D	E	F	G
1							
2		Transactions	Find | View 10 | First 1-39 of 39				
3		Posted Date	Item	Term	Charge	Payment	Refund
4		1/20/2012	Refund - Other	2012 Spring			1,668.00
5			ACCT Course Fee				
6		1/9/2012	- UNDERGRADUATE INTERNSHIP	2012 Spring	51		
7			ENGL Course Fee				
8		1/9/2012	- CREATIVE WRITING I	2012 Spring	-37.5		
9		1/9/2012	Refund - Other	2012 Spring			2,737.00
10		1/6/2012	Direct Stafford Loan	2012 Spring		2,737.00	
11		1/6/2012	Federal Pell Grant	2012 Spring		2,775.00	
12		1/6/2012	M J Harvey Sr Memorial End	2012 Spring		1,000.00	
13		1/6/2012	Texas Public Ed. Grant	2012 Spring		1,000.00	

Excel – Row Adjustment

Repeat

Remember to repeat the Inquiry for each term attended. The

information for separate terms does not have to be separate so you can append it to the previous data, or create separate sheets and generate a total for all terms. The site software does not have a way to select all terms in a particular tax year.

Be careful not to include amounts from terms in other years. Be careful not to omit amounts billed in other years that are paid in the tax year.

These spreadsheet(s) will be used in the next section to calculate the expenses.

Using spreadsheet files is better since the tax preparer can more easily adjust the amounts to categorize and total the expenses, payments, and possible credit.

Tyler Junior College

TJC provides students easy access to their account from their home page.

Login

Go to your browser and enter **http://www.tjc.edu/**

TJC Quick Links

Students can log into their Apache Access account through Quick Links. Click on Quick Links and allow the page to expand the header showing the login window.

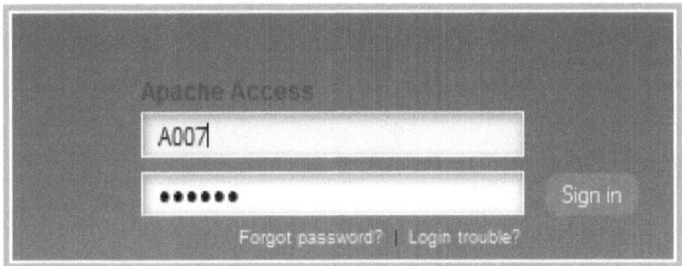

Apache Access – Login

Sign in using the student's ID and password.

Apache Access

This will bring you to a site starting with http://myapacheaccess.tjc.edu/. Click on the Academics tab.

Inquiry

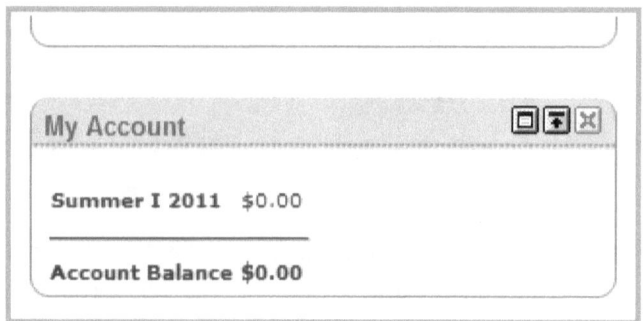

My Account

In the My Account box in the bottom right corner, select the term to view. Some financial data may be shown but you may need to select the more detailed information. Transactions should show dates, amounts, and description.

Plan | Statement and Payment History | Stat

Payment History

At the bottom of the page click Statement and Payment History

erm | Account Detail for Term | Mak

Account Detail

At the bottom of the next screen, click Account Detail for Term

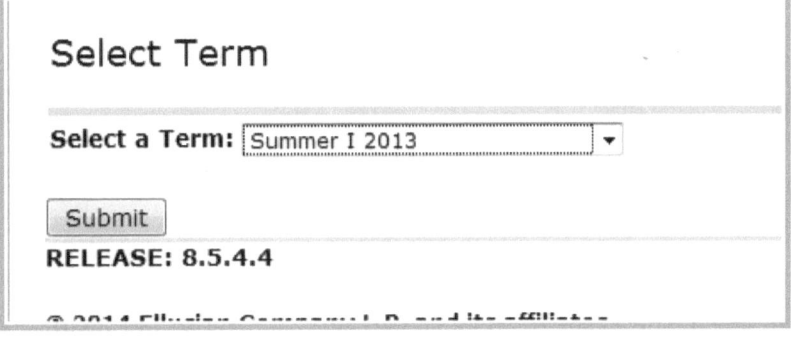

Select Term

201130 Summer I 2011 Term Detail						
Detail Code	**Description**	**Item Date**	**Charge**	**Payment**	**Balance**	Pay Now
DIST	Distance Education Fee	02-JUN-11	$15.00			
HLTF	Health Service Fee	02-JUN-11	$15.00			
LAB	Lab Fees	02-JUN-11	$25.00			
PARK	Parking Fee	02-JUN-11	$15.00			
REG3	Registration Fee	02-JUN-11	$25.00			
GNED	General Education Fee	02-JUN-11	$136.00			
STLF	Student Life Fee	02-JUN-11	$8.00			
TUI1	In-District Tuition	02-JUN-11	$112.00			
DIST	Distance Education Fee	02-JUN-11	-$15.00			
HLTF	Health Service Fee	02-JUN-11	-$15.00			
LAB	Lab Fees	02-JUN-11	-$25.00			
PARK	Parking Fee	02-JUN-11	-$15.00			
REG3	Registration Fee	02-JUN-11	-$25.00			
GNED	General Education Fee	02-JUN-11	-$136.00			
STLF	Student Life Fee	02-JUN-11	-$8.00			
TUI1	In-District Tuition	02-JUN-11	-$112.00			
HLTF	Health Service Fee	02-JUN-11	$15.00			
PARK	Parking Fee	02-JUN-11	$15.00			
REG3	Registration Fee	02-JUN-11	$25.00			
GNED	General Education Fee	02-JUN-11	$102.00			
STLF	Student Life Fee	02-JUN-11	$6.00			
TUI1	In-District Tuition	02-JUN-11	$84.00			
MCV	Mastercard/Visa Payment	12-MAY-11		$247.00		
	Net Term Balance				$0.00	

TJC Term Detail

Then select the term to display the report for the applicable term. Select the items for the term, copy and paste into a spreadsheet. Other display options are available, but make sure dates and description are shown.

In some cases, as illustrated, fees are shown added and then subtracted for classes that are dropped from the original plan. Also note that the amounts in Charges must be categorized to total actual qualifying expenses as will be illustrated in the Calculations section.

Select another term at the bottom for other semesters to make further inquiries.

Student Account Tabulation

This section describes how to categorize and tabulate the relevant amounts for the education credit. Although Treas. Reg. § 1.117-1 says you should exclude scholarships from income to the degree they are used for qualified expenses, Treas. Reg. § 1.25A-5(c) explains how you can manipulate some scholarships to increase the amount of qualified expenses used in calculating an education credit. The best way to determine the amounts to include in income requires some organization of expense and payment records.

Spreadsheet for Expense Calculations

You can spend time verifying and adjusting the amounts on a 1098-T, but taking a few minutes to get an account statement from the college will insure the taxpayer has an accurate record of amounts received and spent. Account records are usually accessible on-line by the student or parent claiming the education credit.

You may be able to mark, copy, and paste the amounts from a web page into a spreadsheet as illustrated in the previous section. Some institutions may even have a way for students to export account information into a downloadable file. The following continues the example for UT Tyler information given above.

Account Record

Date	Item	Term	Charge	Payment	Refund
12/9/2011	BIOL Course Fee - ANATOMY/PHYS...	2012 Spring	61		
12/9/2011	COSC Course Fee - INTERNET & WEB A..	2012 Spring	108		
12/9/2011	Designated Tuition – Undergrad	2012 Spring	2,476		
12/9/2011	Lab Fee - ANATOMY/PHYSIOLOGY LAB II	2012 Spring	5		
12/9/2011	Mandatory Fees - Fall/Spring	2012 Spring	915		
12/9/2011	Resident Tuition	2012 Spring	600		
12/9/2011	Student Services Fee	2012 Spring	132		
12/9/2011	Parking Permit Fall	2012 Spring	30		
12/21/2011	MANA Course Fee - DATABASE INFO S...	2012 Spring	49		
1/6/2012	Direct Stafford Loan	2012 Spring		2,737	
1/6/2012	Federal Pell Grant	2012 Spring		2,775	
1/6/2012	M J Harvey Sr Memorial End	2012 Spring		1,000	

1/6/2012	Texas Public Ed. Grant	2012 Spring	1,000	
1/9/2012	Refund - Other	2012 Spring		2,737
1/20/2012	Refund - Other	2012 Spring		399

In a student account there will usually be two or three columns, Charges, Payments, and possibly Refunds. Once the raw data is pasted into a spreadsheet, you can rename the existing columns to Qualified Expenses, Elective Scholarships, and Loans/Other. Between the first two amount columns, insert columns for Non-Qualified Expenses (the parking permit isn't qualified) and Exclusive Scholarships.

Add separate columns for Taxable Scholarships if applicable and move amounts to their appropriate column. Refund amounts can be grouped with student loans as irrelevant. In this example it is assumed all amounts have actually been paid so we are only categorizing expenses and scholarships. You may only need to move a few amounts as most will probably be qualifying expenses. When complete, add totals to the columns and use those amounts in the following worksheet.

Expense Spreadsheet

Date	Item	Term	Qual Exp	Non Qual	Excl Schps	Electve Schps	Loans/ Other
12/9/2011	BIOL Course Fee - ANATOMY/PHYS...	2012 Spring	61				
12/9/2011	COSC Course Fee - INTERNET & WEB..	2012 Spring	108				
12/9/2011	Designated Tuition - Undergrad	2012 Spring	2,476				
12/9/2011	Lab Fee - ANATOMY/PHYSIOLO L...	2012 Spring	5				
12/9/2011	Mandatory Fees - Fall/Spring	2012 Spring	915				
12/9/2011	Resident Tuition	2012 Spring	600				
12/9/2011	Student Services Fee	2012 Spring	132				
12/9/2012	Parking Permit Fall	2012 Spring		30			
12/21/2012	MANA Course Fee - DATABASE INFO..	2012 Spring	49				
1/6/2012	Direct Stafford Loan	2012 Spring					2,737
1/6/2012	Federal Pell Grant	2012 Spring				2,775	

1/6/2012	M J Harvey Sr Memorial End	2012 Spring				1,000	
1/6/2012	Texas Public Ed. Grant	2012 Spring			1,000		
1/9/2012	Refund - Other	2012 Spring					2,737
1/20/2012	Refund - Other	2012 Spring					399
			4,346	30	1,000	3,775	5,873

Depending on the education credit you are claiming, be sure to add other qualifying expenses, such as required books and other course materials. This should be done even if you have $4,000 in educational expenses since they make that amount of remaining scholarships tax-free. If they are not purchased at the institution, you will have to add them manually.

When querying for the amounts for a school term, be sure to include several months before the start of the term since billing for the spring semester may begin in the previous year, and pay attention to what term the expenses are for. For example, the dates for Spring 2015 might include September 2014 – June 2015.

Expense amounts should be calculated on a term basis, including only terms that start in the tax year. Institutions typically use terms instead of tax years.

Tax Credit Calculation

There are three steps to the calculation of the education credit

1. Determine the amount of qualifying expenses
2. Determine the amount of taxable scholarships
3. Calculating the credit

The amounts are tabulated in the student's college account but must be reconciled to determine the net amount of qualifying expenses for the credit. That is the reason for the AOTC worksheet given below. The third step is primarily a software function, but it is important that preparers know how the 8863 calculations work.

In some cases, calculating the qualifying expenses is as easy as taking the amount in box 1 of Form 1098-T, verifying that with the taxpayer and entering up to $4,000 of that amount on Form 8863. You could subtract scholarships from the box 1 amount and if the amount is $4,000 or more use that on Form 8863. Even when amounts from a Pell grant are included in income to maximize the credit, you can calculate that amount, add it to qualifying expenses and taxable scholarships, and no additional work may be required. That is illustrated in the TaxWise example later. It is when the amount of qualifying expenses is suspect, the calculations are more complex, or the nature of the scholarships is unknown that more work will be involved. For some of those situations you may be able to use the AOTC Worksheet in this section. If more than one type of scholarship was provided this worksheet may be a particularly useful tool.

Calculating Expenses and Scholarships

The key amounts to calculate for education credits are qualifying expenses, scholarships, and the credit based on the net amount of expenses. If the relevant amounts have been exported and tabulated from the student account you can use the following worksheet to calculate the maximum credit amount and the amount of taxable scholarships if any.

Worksheet to Maximize Education Credits

The IRS does have a worksheet for calculating the education credit included in Pub 970 and other sources, but it is used to calculate what can be excluded from income and lacks the logic included in the regulations for elective taxable scholarships. The following worksheet can be used to aid in calculating the maximum AOTC amount.

AOTC Worksheet

A	B	C	D	Formulas for Column D
1	Qualified Expenses	Enter the total amount of your qualified educational expenses.	4,346	
2	Total Scholarships	Enter the total amount of all scholarships and grants received for 2013.	4,775	
3	Taxable Scholarships	Enter the amount of scholarships **required to be used for other than** qualified expenses.	-0-	
4		Subtract line 3 from line 2.	4,775	=D2-D3
5	Excess Scholarships	If line 4 is greater than line 1, subtract line 1 from line 4.	429	=IF(D4>D1,D4-D1,0)
6	Potential Tax-free Scholarships	Subtract line 5 from line 4	4,346	=D4-D5
7	Exclusive Scholarships	Enter the amount of the scholarships that you are **required to use** for qualified educational expenses.	1,000	
8	Elective Scholarships	If line 6 is greater than line 7, Subtract line 7 from line 6.	3,346	=IF(D6>D7,D6-D7,0)
9	Excess Expenses Paid by Taxpayer	If line 1 is greater than line 6, Subtract line 6 from line 1	-0-	=IF(D1>D6,D1-D6,0)
10	Qualified Expenses for Tax Credit	Add line 8 and line 9 (maximum 4000). Enter this amount on **line 27 of Form 8863**.	3,346	=MIN(4000, D9+D8)
11	Elective Scholarships Includable in Income	If line 9 is less than line 10, subtract line 9 from line 10. Otherwise, enter 0.	3,346	=IF(D10>D9,D10-D9,0)
12	Total Scholarships Included in Income	Add line 3, line 5 and line 11. This is the amount of taxable scholarships. Enter SCH and this amount on the dotted line to the left of line 7. Include this amount in the total on **line 7 of Form 1040**.	3,775	=D3+D5+D11

Column and row headings are shown and Excel Formulas are given in the final column. If using a spreadsheet, you may want to include a process in your workflow to link the totals from the calculations to the appropriate cells in the spreadsheet. Notice that you only have to enter four amounts (if applicable) in the worksheet to calculate the amounts needed for the tax return. A self-calculating PDF version of the worksheet can be downloaded at

www.tylerhosting.com/EdCredit/.

This worksheet assumes the taxpayer does not have any outstanding balances, and does not consider other educational assistance, or the possibility of excluding qualified expenses of other types of financial aid. It can be expanded or condensed to suit the needs of the practitioner. With more complex arrangements additional research and manipulation may be necessary. The Special Issues section includes some items to consider with education credits, including its effect on EITC or financial aid, for example.

The AOTC worksheet is only a tool and may not be enough for some circumstances. The preparer must understand the law to know what modifications may be needed for extraneous information. If Coverdell or Section 529 accounts are used you might be able to reduce qualifying expenses by the amount and continue with the worksheet. This worksheet (or the PDF) can also be saved with the work-papers to document the calculation. In many cases, only a few numbers will be used in the calculations. Exclusive and taxable scholarships may never be a part of the computation.

Remember that scholarship amounts that cover services rendered such as teaching or research are normally considered taxable earned income, not scholarship income, and would not enter into the calculations.

IRS Scenarios
Below are scenarios illustrated in examples from Publication 970 and Treas. Reg. § 1.25A-5. The worksheet following demonstrates the use of the worksheet for these scenarios.

970-1: Bill Pass, age 28 and unmarried, enrolled full-time in 2013 as a first-year student at a local college to earn a degree in law enforcement. This was his first year of post-secondary education. During 2013, he paid $5,600 for his qualified education expenses and $4,400 for his room and board for the fall 2013 semester. He and the college meet all the requirements for the American opportunity credit. He figures his American opportunity credit based on qualified education expenses of $4,000, which results in a credit of $2,500.

970-3: The facts are the same as in 970-1, except that Bill was awarded a $5,600 scholarship. Under the terms of his scholarship, it may be used to pay any educational expenses, including room and board. If Bill includes $4,000 of the scholarship in income, he will be deemed to have used that amount to pay for room and board. The remaining $1,600 of the $5,600 scholarship will reduce his qualified education expenses and his adjusted qualified education expenses will be $4,000. Based on his adjusted qualified education expenses of $4,000, Bill would be able to claim an American opportunity tax credit of $2,500.

25A-2: University X charges Student A, who lives on University X's campus, $3,000 for tuition and $5,000 for room and board. University X awards Student A a $2,000 scholarship. The terms of the scholarship permit it to be used to pay any of a student's costs of attendance at University X, including tuition, room and board, and other incidental expenses. University X applies the $2,000 scholarship against Student A's $8,000 total bill, and Student A pays the $6,000 balance of her bill from University X with a combination of savings and amounts she earns.

Student A reports the entire scholarship as income on the student's federal income tax return. Therefore, for purposes of calculating an education tax credit, Student A is treated as having paid $3,000 of qualified tuition and related expenses to University X.

25A-4: The facts are the same as in 25A-2, except that the terms of the scholarship require it to be used to pay tuition or room and board charged by University X, and the scholarship amount is $6,000. Student A may allocate the scholarship between tuition and room and board in any manner. However, because room and board totals $5,000 that is the maximum amount that can be applied under the terms of the scholarship to expenses other than qualified expenses and at least $1,000 of the scholarship must be applied to tuition. If Student A reports $5,000 of the scholarship as income on the student's federal income tax return, then Student A will be treated as having paid $2,000 ($3,000 tuition–$1,000 qualified scholarship excludable under section 117) in qualified tuition and related expenses to University X.

AOTC Worksheet – IRS Examples

			970-1	970-3	25A-2	25A-4
1	Qualified Expenses	Enter the total amount of your qualified educational expenses.	5600	5600	3000	3000
2	Total Scholarships	Enter the total amount of all scholarships and grants received for 2013.	0	5600	2000	6000
3	Taxable Scholarships	Enter the amount of scholarships **required to be used for other than** qualified expenses.				5000
4		Subtract line 3 from line 2.	0	5600	2000	1000
5	Excess Scholarships	If line 4 is greater than line 1, subtract line 1 from line 4.	0	0	0	0
6	Potential Tax-free Scholarships	Subtract line 5 from line 4	0	5600	2000	1000
7	Exclusive Scholarships	Enter the amount of the scholarships that you are **required to use** for qualified educational expenses.				1000
8	Elective Scholarships	If line 6 is greater than line 7, Subtract line 7 from line 6.	0	5600	2000	0
9	Excess Expenses Paid by Taxpayer	If line 1 is greater than line 6, Subtract line 6 from line 1	5600	0	1000	2000
10	Qualified Expenses for Tax Credit	Add line 8 and line 9 (maximum 4000). Enter this amount on **line 27 of Form 8863.**	4000	4000	3000	2000

11	Elective Scholarships Includable in Income	If line 9 is less than line 10, subtract line 9 from line 10. Otherwise, enter 0.	0	4000	2000	0
12	Total Scholarships Included in Income	Add line 3, line 5 and line 11. This is the amount of taxable scholarship. Enter SCH and this amount on the dotted line to the left of line 7. Include this amount in the total on **line 7 of Form 1040.**	0	4000	2000	5000

Understanding Form 8863

The lengthy form 8863 can be confusing, but the computations are really basic for most tax returns. Preparers will usually not need to use the form itself other than entering the qualifying expenses on page 2. The software usually does the rest. However, if the preparer reviews each page of the return with the taxpayer knowing how it works will be important.

The 8863 consists of two pages. As is often the case with IRS forms, page 2 is completed prior to completing page 1. There is only one 8863 per return, but if there are more than one student, there should be a page 2 of the form for each student showing student and institution information. It has four qualifications questions, qualifying expenses, and the initial calculation of the available credit. As the law directs, the credit is 100% of the first $2,000 and 25% of the second $2,000, and that is what the last section of part III calculates. This is the maximum credit allowed for your expenses.

The amounts from page 2 carry over to page 1 where the actual credit is calculated. There is a side calculation that adjusts for the phase-out. If line 6 is not a 1.000 then you can explain to the taxpayer that their credit is subject to the phase-out and explain the income levels being used. Then it calculates the refundable portion of the credit at 40% of the amount calculated at line 7. That is then subtracted from the line 7 amount to get the remainder which is the maximum nonrefundable credit portion. The nonrefundable portion is limited to taxable income after adjusting for a couple of other credits.

The education credit shows up on the 1040 on two separate lines. The nonrefundable credit shows in the credit section on the second page of Form 1040 (or variant) while the refundable credit shows in the payments section.

Phase-out Calculations

The completion of Form 8863 may be more involved if the taxpayer is in the phase-out range for the AOTC. Tax software generally does that calculation but understanding how it is calculated may assist in deciding whether to and how much of scholarships to include in income. The phase-out is essentially based on percentage of income between lower and upper phase-out limits. Thus, $1000 over (based on $10,000 range) would reduce your credit by 10%.

If you happen to be put into the phase-out range by including scholarships and grants in income, re-calculate the credit omitting some or all of the scholarships to determine the most advantageous treatment. Generally, it will be most advantageous to include the first $2000 of expenses regardless of including scholarships in income. Above the first $2000, the net benefit will largely depend on your marginal tax rate, deductions, and the amount of tax owed.

Maximizing the Lifetime Learning Credit

The Lifetime Learning Credit may be available to students that do not qualify for AOTC. After the first four years of college some students will need to convert to using the LLC. Although it is non-refundable, tax liability can be lowered by claiming the LLC. If there is more than 10,000 in expenses and scholarships are not a factor, simply claim it all.

Similar to the AOTC you can include scholarships in income to increase the credit. but the calculation of the maximum credit require a different approach. This would be considered when the credit amount is less than the tax.

Consider the scenario where the taxpayer has a tax bill of $1,000, $12,000 qualifying expenses, paid by an $8,000 scholarship and $4,000 he paid in cash. Without any adjustments, his LLC credit amount would be $800 ($4,000 * 20%) leaving a $200 tax bill remaining. If the taxpayer includes $2,000 of elective scholarships in income, he will increase his tax bill by $200 (at 10% marginal tax rate), increase his qualifying expenses by $2,000 (to $6,000), and increase his credit by $400 to $1,200, leaving a zero tax bill. This is only the maximum amount for scholarship inclusion; Items such as EITC could affect the total calculation.

One way to get a ballpark figure for the amount of scholarships to add to income is to take the remaining tax and multiply by 10. In the example just given, the remaining tax was $200 so $2,000 of scholarships were added to income. This is a ballpark figure, so it will be necessary to verify with the actual calculation.

In some cases, you can determine the range where the benefit ends by comparing the benefit with the marginal tax bracket. This is particularly true if the tax liability is considerable higher than the potential credit. Find the tax bracket margin where tax rate changes from 15% to 25%, which is the highest amount that is taxable at 15%. Anything above that would be taxed at 25%. Scholarships included in income will be taxed at the marginal tax bracket. Since the credit is only 20%, you would lose money by including scholarships in income above that income level.

Tax Preparation Techniques

Knowing how to process a particular return with potential education credits will save a considerable amount of time. In some cases you will not need to go to the trouble of completing a worksheet.

In many cases claiming the education credit for clients is relatively easy. If there are only taxpayer expenses you only need to determine the amount of qualifying expenses (QE). In many cases that is reported on the 1098-T. Add required expenses paid elsewhere and the rest is math. It becomes just a little more difficult if scholarships are involved. In those cases you need to determine the amount of QE and coordinate that with scholarships. Normally scholarships offset QE and you would take the difference. If some amount of scholarship covered expenses is included in QE you simply need to remember to include that amount in taxable scholarships. Following are a few scenarios to consider.

Simple

If expenses exceed scholarships by more than $4,000, no calculations are necessary. The qualifying expenses are $4,000 and no scholarships are taxable unless they are for non-qualifying expenses.

Elective

If expenses exceed $4,000 and expenses are more than scholarships then you can often take the difference as the initial amount of qualifying expenses. If the initial amount is less than $4,000 and the taxpayer is below the 25% tax bracket you will usually want to include scholarships in income and qualifying expenses until you have $4,000 in qualifying expenses.

If the initial amount is less than $2,000 and the taxpayer is in a tax bracket above 25% then you may only want to include enough to get $2,000 in qualifying expenses. If the initial amount is $2,000 or more and the taxpayer is in a tax bracket above 25% then it will not be beneficial to increase the credit by including scholarships in income.

The alignment of the tax brackets and AOTC qualifications are currently such that qualifying single taxpayers will rarely be above the 25% tax bracket, although married filers may be.

Excess Complications

When scholarships exceed expenses then the calculation is a little more advanced. If expenses exceed $4,000, but scholarships are more than expenses, include excess scholarships in income, plus $2,000 of the elective scholarships. If there is still taxable income and the taxpayer's marginal tax bracket is less than 25%, include scholarship in income (up to $2,000) to increase the credit until tax is zero.

Family Coordination

One of the quirks to be aware of when preparing returns with education credits involves coordinating returns of the taxpayer and student. If the taxpayer claims an education credit based on including scholarships in income, it is the student (not the taxpayer) that must include the scholarship in his income. The paid expenses can be moved back and forth depending on who claims the credit, but the scholarships can't. Like many situations when the parent may or may not claim a child, the returns should be coordinated for the most benefit.

One factor to consider is the refundable nature of the credit. If fully nonrefundable, the credit is 100% of the first $2000 and 25% of the next $1000. If the credit is refundable the credit is only 40% of that amount, so the values to consider change. In other words, the refundable credit is 40% of the first $2000 and 10% (40% * 25%) of the next $2000. This 10% is important because if a student must include taxable scholarships in income and it is taxable, the minimum tax rate would be 10%, so the credit is wiped out by that portion of the credit. The student may not want to pay tax on scholarship just to shift that same amount to the parent's credit. If EITC is involved, there may even be a net loss on the claim. Consider the following scenarios.

Parent is claiming the student and the AOTC. Their tax before the credit is $900 and they are in the 15% tax bracket. Qualifying expenses are $6,000. Elective scholarships are $3,500. Net qualifying expenses are then $2,500. Student AGI is $5,500. Parent has the option of claiming on the $2,500 and up to $1500 of the scholarships included in income.

Decision 1: If the parent claims only the $2,500 then their potential credit will be $2,000 + $125 ($500 * 25%) = $2,125. The refundable portion is 40% of that amount ($850) and the nonrefundable portion is limited by their tax ($900). Their total credit is $850 + $900 = $1,750. The student will not owe any tax.

Decision 2: If the parent claims the total $4,000, then the student must include $1500 in income. The potential credit for the parent will then be $2,500. They will receive the refundable amount of $1,000 plus the $900 amount of tax owed for a total of $1,900. Since the student must then add the extra $1,500 to his income, his AGI is now $7,000. The student's taxable bill will then be $80 (($7000 - $6200) * 10%). The net effect is a $1,820 ($1,900 - $80) credit.

Decision 3: If we reduce the taxable scholarships to $700 then the parent's potential credit would be $2,300, composed of the $920 refundable credit and $1,380 nonrefundable credit. The actual credit will be the $920 plus the $900 of tax for a total of $1,820. The student will have income of only $6200, none of which is taxable income.

A different set of circumstances will exist if the tax owed is more than the nonrefundable portion of the credit or the student owes tax before adjustments. To continue this exercise, assume that the parent's tax before the credit is $1,500 and they are in the 15% tax bracket. Qualifying expenses are $6,000. Elective scholarships are $3,500. Net qualifying expenses are then $2,500. Student AGI is $5,500.

Decision 1: If the parent claims only the $2,500 then their potential credit will be $2,000 + $125 ($500 * 25%) = $2,125. The refundable portion is 40% of that amount ($850) and the nonrefundable portion is $1,275. Their total credit is $850 + $1,275 = $2,125. The student will not owe any tax.

Decision 2: If the parent claims the total $4,000, then the student must include $1500 in income. The potential credit for the parent will then be $2,500. They will receive the refundable amount of $1,000 plus the $1,500 amount of tax owed for a total of $2,500. Since the student must then add the extra $1,500 to his income, his AGI is now $7,000. The student's taxable bill will then be $80 (($7000 - $6200) * 10%). The net effect is a $2,420 ($2,500 - $80) credit.

Decision 3: If we reduce the taxable scholarships to $700 then the parent's credit would be $2,300. The student will have income of only $6200, none of which is taxable income.

In this case, Decision 2 provides the highest net benefit.

The best way to proceed may be to prepare the student's return first, allowing the parent to claim on $2000. Then evaluate the taxable income of the student. If below $6,200, add scholarships up to total $6,200. If parent's tax is more than the credit, increase the credit to cover that tax (credit at 40%), and add that amount to the student's taxable income (taxed at 10%). For the second $2,000, if there is no tax on which to use the nonrefundable credit, then re-characterizing the scholarships to claim the refundable credit would be a wash.

Keep in mind that other factors may need to be considered, such as changes in EITC due to AGI. Scholarships are not earned income but the EITC is calculated on both earned income and AGI. The lowest EITC table amount is the amount of the EITC credit. Also, the AOTC credit may be reduced by other credits being claimed on the return.

Avoiding Family Conflict

One of the difficulties in family coordination is that the student may be increasing his taxable income, while the parent is enjoying the credit. In order to avoid family conflict it may be advisable to recommend filing Form 8888 to allocate part of the refund to the student by depositing an amount that offsets the students sacrifice.

Alternately the parent could allow the student to do a direct debit from the parent's account for his tax liability due to taxable scholarships. This is not always possible, such as when there is a tax reduction but no refund amount. Ultimately, the taxpayer and student will have to agree on the process before claiming the credit on the student's scholarship inclusion.

Note that the regulations indicate that qualifying expenses can be increased if scholarships are included in income, so scholarship inclusion is the prerequisite. Claiming the credit doesn't require the student to include scholarships in income. Scholarship inclusion is required before the taxpayer can claim the credit. If, however, the student is not required to file a return after considering scholarship inclusion, the taxpayer can assume the amounts have been included in income.

Tax Bracket Watch

When attempting to maximize the credit a good guide is to remember the percentages of each part of the credit. The nonrefundable portion is 100% of the first $2,000, and 25% of the next $2,000. If you are over the 25% tax bracket, then it may be better not include scholarships in income to claim the second $2,000. Similarly the refundable portion amounts to 40% of the first $2,000 and 10% of the second $2,000. For this portion the break-even tax bracket is 10%.

Software Solutions

Now that you understand the law and education credit opportunities, you now need to enter the information into your tax software. This may be one of the hurdles to getting more preparers to consider elective scholarships in education credits.

The following sections review the entries in the more popular packages. Other than TaxWise my observations are based on prior year versions of the software as noted. In some cases, the software will evaluate the credits and deductions and select the most favorable one, but I have yet to review a software package that assists or naturally supports scholarship inclusion to maximize education credits. It is up to the preparer to calculate and code the information appropriately.

These are simple examples. If the calculations require using the AOTC Worksheet to determine the amount, use the appropriate amounts from that form. Practically all tax software requires you to enter information for the institution and answer questions related to qualifications for the education credit. If the software does not provide input of scholarships from the 1098-T then the expenses entered should be net of those scholarships.

Software Based Negligence

Tax software is a blessing to tax professionals. Much of tax preparation can be done by simply transferring information from client provided tax forms to the computer and letting the software do all of the work. The downside of that is that many preparers and assistants do not question the proper recording of amounts, and form calculations.

In the case of education credits, tax software is often lacking. For example, software will typically flag items that need completion when partial information is entered during an interview. The TaxWise software that is used to prepare tax returns in the IRS VITA/TCE programs does not flag the 8863 for completion when only entering part of the information for the credit. It is often necessary to manually select and complete all of the required forms and fields to complete an education credit claim. In contrast, TaxWise does flag EITC and requires completion before it passes diagnostic tests.

Similarly, Lacerte does not have a specific field to enter scholarships received on a Form 1098-T and Intuit on-line help provides several manual solutions for this issue.[16] The lack of support for all aspects of education credit claims is the reason for this section. The important thing to note is that you should not assume the credit does not apply simply because the software does not automatically calculate it.

1098-T Analysis and Inquiry

Before entering the information it is important to analyze and verify the source documents, particularly the 1098-T. Look at the form and ask appropriate questions. When someone comes in with a 1098-T the first thing you should do is look at the half-time box. If that is not checked and the form is correct, then that student doesn't qualify for AOTC, but they may qualify for the Lifetime Learning Credit.

When examining the 1098-T remember that the form may not be accurate. The instructions for the form are limited and do not fully reflect the requirements of the law. For example, the graduate student box may checked only because the student was a graduate student at the end of the year. Likewise, the half-time box may be checked because the student was less than half-time the final semester of the year. In both cases the student may still qualify for the credit. The amount of qualifying expenses may also be inaccurate. Verify questionable entries by examining the student's financial records.

Next, see how the expenses are reported on the form. Institutions can report amounts received on amounts billed or amounts actually paid. If box 3 or box 7 is checked, taxpayer will need to provide additional information. If box 7 is checked the amounts shown may

---

16 https://accountants.intuit.com/support/tax/lacerte/document.jsp?
    product=lacerte&id=GEN68250&inproduct=true

include amounts not paid. Even if box 7 is not checked, the amounts may not be accurate if some amounts paid during the tax year were billed in the previous year. If amounts billed for first three months of the next year were actually paid, then the taxpayer can include them in qualifying expenses. Generally scholarships and grants are not paid in advance.

In all cases verify the amounts paid and from what sources. Ask what expenses were paid. Normally all expenses would have been paid if they do not owe the school. Amounts paid by check or through school loans are considered amounts paid. Although I prefer to get account information from the school records, you can rely on the information provided by the taxpayer if it is reasonable. If you don't have account information from the school or a 1098-T you should probably not file for education credits. Claiming education tax credits without proof has been a common method of tax fraud.

Finally, ask about books and computer expenses that may not be on the 1098-T. If they are required expenses they can include them as qualifying expenses paid.

You might ask about use of Coverdell ESA or Roth IRA funds used to pay expenses. This money is tax-free and can cover room and board. Normally you would subtract room and board from this amount (Don't add to qualifying expenses) and subtract the remaining from QE or include in income. A penalty exception applies for IRA distributions. Education Savings Accounts, IRAs for education, and other forms of assistance are discussed later.

TaxWise

This is a brief set of instructions for reporting education credits in TaxWise to assist in preparing most returns with AOTC. The process is pretty simple and will be very similar in other tax packages. While TaxWise does require entry of student information and institution information, it doesn't have a 1098-T form in the software. In order to explain the calculations, consider the following example:

Example 1: Student has $7,000 in expenses (paid) and scholarships of $5,250 (all from a Pell grant). Box 7 is not checked. He also purchased $720 in books from an on-line retailer.

Preliminary Calculations

Total and enter the information in 8863 including the amount of qualifying expenses. If none of the expenses are paid with scholarships and grants, you can include all expenses on 8863 and you should be finished with preliminaries. If scholarships are reported, you will need to offset expenses with those scholarships. Subtract scholarships from expenses to get initial Qualifying Expenses and enter that amount on 8863. If several items will be included in expenses, you will want to use a scratchpad to identify each one. In this example, $7,000 – $5,250 = $1,750 expenses would initially be entered for qualified education expenses.

	Detail Sheet	2014
Name: BRILLIANT STUDENT		SSN: 123-33-2029
Description:	EDUCATION CREDIT	
Type		Amount
OUT OF POCKET EXPENSES ▷		1750
		0
		0
		0
		0
		0

Qualified Expenses – Scratch Pad

American Opportunity Credit

27	Adjusted qualified education expenses. See instructions - do not enter more than $4,000	1750
28	Subtract $2,000 from line 27, but not less than -0-	0▶
29	Multiply line 28 by 25%	0
30	If line 28 is -0-, amount from line 27. Otherwise, add $2,000 to the amount on line 29. Skip line 31	1750

Qualified Expenses – Form 8863

Entering Other Expenses

If books were not purchased from the institution (AOTC only) add that to qualifying expenses at this point. The initial expenses plus the $720 for books brings the total to $2,470 as reflected on the 8863.

Type	Amount
OUT OF POCKET EXPENSES	1750
BOOKS	720
	0
	0
	0
	0
	0
	0

Qualified Expenses – Books Added

American Opportunity Credit

27	Adjusted qualified education expenses. See instructions - do not enter more than $4,000	2470
28	Subtract $2,000 from line 27, but not less than -0-	470
29	Multiply line 28 by 25%	118▶
30	If line 28 is -0-, amount from line 27. Otherwise, add $2,000 to the amount on line 29. Skip line 31	2118

Qualified Expenses – Updated Form 8863

Scholarship Adjustments

Ask the taxpayer about the nature of the scholarships. If the scholarships include Pell grants, add enough Pell grant money to the expenses in order to bring the total to $4,000. In this case, $4,000 minus the initial $2,470 equals $1,530. We enter that amount first to qualified expenses.

Type	Amount
OUT OF POCKET EXPENSES	1750
BOOKS	720
EXPENSE FROM SCHOLARSHIPS INCLUDED IN INCOME	1530
	0
	0
	0

Qualified Expenses – Scholarship Adjustment

American Opportunity Credit

27	Adjusted qualified education expenses. See instructions - do not enter more than $4,000	4000
28	Subtract $2,000 from line 27, but not less than -0-	2000▶
29	Multiply line 28 by 25%	500
30	If line 28 is -0-, amount from line 27. Otherwise, add $2,000 to the amount on line 29. Skip line 31	2500

Qualified Expenses – Updated Form 8863

Note: If the amount of the Pell grant is less than the amount calculated, only add that amount to the expenses and adjust the total accordingly.

Adding Scholarship Income

Then you need to add the same amount to Form 1040 Line 7 scholarships. You will need to use the second line on the form and link to a scratch pad. This amount must be identified as scholarships. If it is just included in the Line 7 total, then it would be incorrectly be added to earned income for EITC.

	Detail Sheet		2014
Name: BRILLIANT STUDENT		SSN: 123-33-2029	

Description:	TAXABLE SCHOLARSHIP INCLUDED	
Type		Amount
SCHOLARSHIP INCLUDED TO MAXIMIZE EDUCATION CREDIT	▶	1530
		0
		0

Taxable Scholarship – Scratch Pad

Income								
7	Wages, salaries, tips, etc.	AB ☐	FB ☐	DCB ☐	SNE ☐	SSHIP ☑		1530
	Taxable scholarship not on Form W2					1530		
	Household employee income not on Form W2					0		
8a	Taxable interest							0
b	Tax-exempt interest					0		
9a	Ordinary dividends including qualified dividends from Forms 8814,							
	listed on Schedule B _____ 0							0
b	Qualified dividends including qualified dividends from Forms 8814,							
	listed on Schedule B _____ 0							

Taxable Scholarship – Form 1040 Line 7

Excess scholarships

Now let's assume that the student has scholarships in excess of expenses. The process is the same except that you initially include the excess scholarships in income instead of including expenses on 8863. The following example illustrates the process in this case.

Example 2: Student has $7,000 in expenses and $9,000 in scholarships and grants (including a $5,250 Pell grant). She also purchased $720 in books from an on-line retailer.

If scholarships are greater than expenses subtract the expenses from scholarships to get the amount of taxable scholarships. If we assume the student had $9,000 in scholarships and $7,000 in expenses she would include $2,000 ($9,000 – $7,000) in taxable scholarship income as excess scholarships. Next, she would include any expenses not included on the 1098-T such as the $720 in books as qualifying expenses on the 8863. Finally, she would calculate and include enough of the Pell grant in expenses ($4,000 - $720 = $3,280) to maximize AOTC expenses.

However, in this example another issue needs to be addressed. Since there was an excess amount of scholarships, the amount of elective scholarships should be reduced by that amount. The maximizing amount for the credit is $3,280, but the elective amount of the Pell grant is now $5,250 - $2,000 = $3,250 so that limits the amount to add to qualifying expenses and taxable scholarships. The amount $3,250 is now added to both qualifying expenses and taxable scholarships. If using the AOTC worksheet covered elsewhere this issue is resolved automatically. The AOTC worksheet could also be completed and used as the primary input source. The following screen-shots show the completed forms for this example.

Type	Amount
BOOKS PURCHASED OUT OF POCKET ▷	720
EXPENSES FROM SCHOLARSHIPS INCLUDED IN INCOME	3250
	0
	0
	0
	0
	0

Qualified Expenses – Scratch Pad

American Opportunity Credit

27	Adjusted qualified education expenses. See instructions - do not enter more than $4,000	3970
28	Subtract $2,000 from line 27, but not less than -0-	1970
29	Multiply line 28 by 25%	493
30	If line 28 is -0-, amount from line 27. Otherwise, add $2,000 to the amount on line 29. Skip line 31	2493

Qualified Expenses – Form 8863

Then add the same amount to scholarship income.

Type	Amount
EXCESS SCHOLARSHIPS	2000
SCHOLARSHIPS INCLUDED TO MAXIMIZE EDUCATION CREDIT	3250
	0
▷	0
	0
	0
	0
	0
	0

Taxable Scholarship – Scratch Pad

Income

7	Wages, salaries, tips, etc. AB ☐ FB ☐ DCB ☐ SNE ☐ SSHIP ☑			5250
	Taxable scholarship not on Form W2		5250	
	Household employee income not on Form W2		0	
8a	Taxable interest			0
b	Tax-exempt interest		0	
9a	Ordinary dividends including qualified dividends from Forms 8814, listed on Schedule B _____ 0			0

Taxable Scholarship – Form 1040 Line 7

These examples illustrate the treatment of Pell grants. Other scholarships might be able to be treated the same way, but it will require knowing the terms of the scholarship. Note: If scholarships are reported on W-2, report as W-2 earnings. Don't make adjustment to QE or taxable scholarships.

Intuit Pro Series (2012)

Pro Series attempts to assist in the calculation of qualifying expenses by providing a 1098-T form to enter the amounts being used but it doesn't directly allow you to allocate some scholarships to income. While it attempts to be helpful, it can also be frustrating to find the correct form to enter the information.

Pro Series features a QuickZoom on certain pages that allow the preparer to link to related forms. Because ProSeries 2012 did not list forms in tree form, it becomes more difficult to navigate the forms being used for the Education Credit. Consider the following structure when navigating in Pro Series.

Education Costs (Education Tuition and Fees Summary)

- Student Worksheet(s)
  - 1098-T
- 8863

Many boxes also support a supporting statement screen. Note that there may be an 8863 page 2 for each student, but only once 8863 page 1 for the return.

Example 1: Student has 7,000 in expenses (billed) and scholarships of 5,250 (all from a Pell grant). Box 7 is not checked. He purchased 720 in books from an on-line retailer.

Preliminary Entries

Start an education credit in several ways, but the easiest way to find related forms is to start with Education in the Common Forms section.

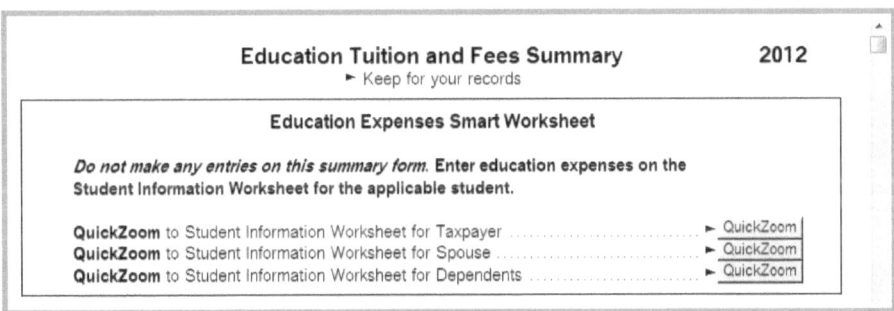

Common Forms – Education

From that sheet, select the appropriate Student Information Worksheet to begin entering the information.

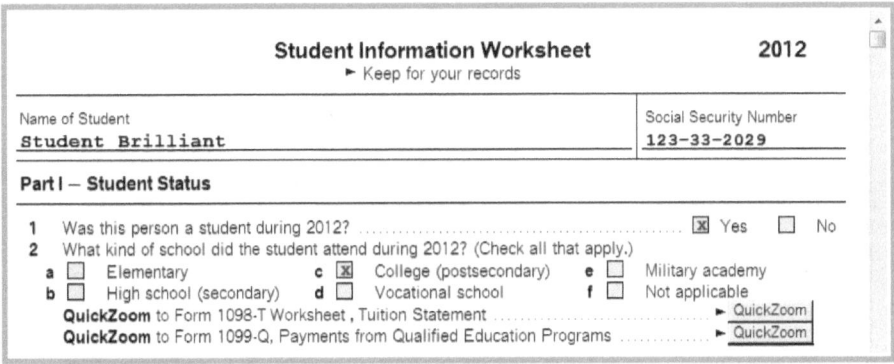

Student Information Worksheet

After completing the worksheet through Part 3, select QuickZoom to Form 1098-T and complete Part I as reported on the 1098-T. When possible identify the items (e.g. Pell grants) included in scholarships for future reference.

1098-T Worksheet	Tuition Statement ► Keep for your records	2012

Taxpayer's name **Student Brilliant**	Social Security No. **123-33-2029**

1098-T Information (Required):

A A Form 1098-T was received from this institution .... Yes ☒   No ☐

B A Form 1098-T was received from this institution in **2011** with Box 2 filled in and
   Box 7 checked .... Yes ☐   No ☒

Identify Student (Required):

A If student is   **Student**
   Check to indicate student .... ► ☒ Taxpayer ☐ Spouse

B If student is
   Double-click to link this 1098-T to the applicable *Dependent Student*
   Information Worksheet .... ►

Filer's name **UT Tyler**	**1** Payments received for qualified tuition and related expenses .... $ **7,000.**
Street address **3900 Univ Blvd**	
City State Zip Code **Tyler** **TX** **75799**	**2** Amounts billed for qualified tuition and related expenses .... $
Foreign province/county	**3** If this box is checked, your educational institution has changed its reporting method for 2012 .... ☐
Foreign postal code Foreign country	

Filer's Federal identification number **11-1111111**	Student's Social Security Number. **123-33-2029**	**4** Adjustments made for a prior year $	**5** Scholarships or grants $ **5,250.**

1098-T Worksheet

Identify the amounts included in the worksheet by adding a supporting statement.

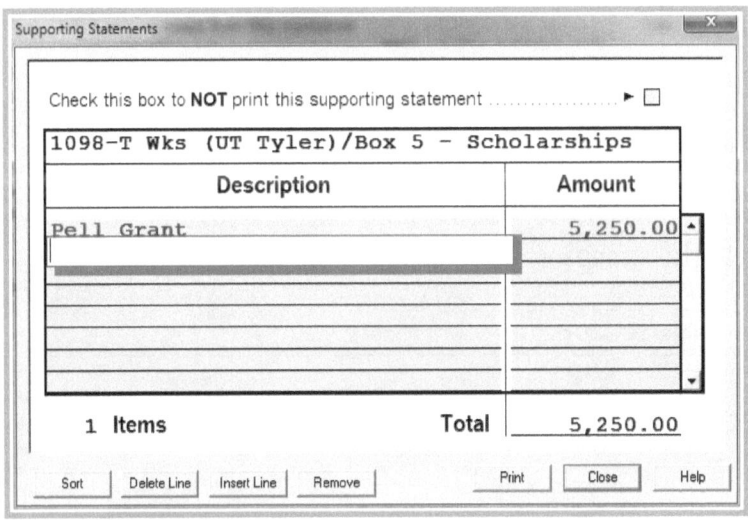

1098-T Worksheet – Supporting Statement

Part IV – Educational Institution and Tuition Summary					
		Received 2011 1098T with Box 2 filled and box 7 checked?			
School Name EIN	Address (number, street, apt no., city, state, and ZIP Code)	Tuition paid	Scholar- ships or grants	On Form 1098-T	
UT Tyler 11-1111111 If a foreign address: foreign province/state: Postal code: Country:	3900 Univ Blvd Tyler TX 75799	7,000.	5,250.	Yes ☒ No ☐	Yes ☐ No ☒
If a foreign address: foreign province/state: Postal code: Country:				Yes ☐ No ☐	Yes ☐ No ☐
Totals		7,000.	5,250.		

Updated Student Information Worksheet

Pro Series Help advises that a 1098-T form should be completed for all students even if an actual 1098-T was not received. This information is linked to the same information required on Form 8863. The bottom of the 1098-T form allows you to modify the 1098-T amounts for qualifying expenses paid but don't adjust expenses just yet. Return to Student Information Worksheet and notice that the 1098-T information has been included in Part IV. Skip Part V until later.

Entering Other Expenses

Now complete Part VI. This is where books and other expenses not paid to the institution can be entered. The $720 in books has been added to the expenses.

Part VI — Education Expenses									
Description	Total	Amount eligible for							
		American Opportunity Credit **Not Qualified**	Lifetime Learning Credit **Not Qualified**	Tuition and Fees Deduction **Not Qualified**	Qualified Higher Education Expense for 529 Plan **Not Applicable**	Qualified Higher Education Expense for ESA **Not Applicable**	Qualified Higher Education Expense for US Bonds **Not Applicable**	Qualified Elementary and Secondary Expense for ESA **Not Applicable**
Expenses:									
1 Tuition paid from Part IV....	7,000.	7,000.	7,000.	7,000.				
Paid to institution as a condition of enrollment:									
2 Fees									
3 Books, supplies, equipment									
Paid to other than institution or not a condition of enrollment:									
4 Books, supplies, equipment	720.	720						
5 Other course-related									
6 Room and board...........									
7 Special needs expenses									
8 Computer expenses									
9 QTP or ESA contribution ..									
10 Academic tutoring									
11 Uniforms									
12 Transportation									
13 Total qualified expenses	7,720.	7,720.	7,000.	7,000.				

Student Information Worksheet – Additional Expenses

Review the 1098-T and reconcile the amounts actually paid if necessary.

Reconciliation of Box 1, Payments Received for Qualified Tuition and Related Expenses	
A Enter box 1 amount **not** paid during 2012	0.
B Enter box 1 amount actually paid during 2012	7,000.

Reconciliation of Box 2, Amounts Billed for Qualified Tuition and Related Expenses	
A Enter box 2 amount **not** paid during 2012	
B Enter box 2 amount actually paid during 2012	

Reconciliation of Box 5, Veteran- or Employer-Provided Assistance Included in Box 5	
A Enter portion of box 5 amount from veteran- or tax free employer-provided assistance	
B Enter portion of box 5 amount from employer-provided assistance included in income	
C Portion of box 5 amount from scholarships or grants	5,250.

Expense Reconciliation

One of the flaws inherent in using a 1098-T is that it assumes correct 1098-T amounts, and this package doesn't provide any alerts when some of the amounts are for the following year. You may need to change the amount for Box 1 of the 1098-T. Use the reconciliation section for Box 1 to show the actual amounts paid.

Scholarship Adjustments

Form 8863, page 2, line 27 should now show the tentative amount of qualifying expenses. Note: This is a total for all students.

If line 27 does not show $4,000 (for one student), consider possible adjustments. In this case Form 8863 shows $2,470. The difference between $2,470 and $4,000 is $1,530. Pell grants are more than $1,530 so we can include that amount in income and increase qualifying expenses.

American Opportunity Credit		
27 Adjusted qualified education expenses. **Do not enter more than $4,000**	27	2,470.
28 Subtract $2,000 from line 27. If zero or less enter -0-	28	470.
29 Multiply line 28 by 25% (.25)	29	118.
30 If line 28 is zero, enter the amount from line 27. Otherwise, add $2,000 to the amount on line 29 and enter the result. Skip line 31. Include the total of all amounts from all Part III, line 30 on Part 1, line 1	30	2,118.

Initial Form 8863

Go to Student Information worksheet. Under Scholarships, other, enter -1530. You can use a supporting worksheet to identify that amount.

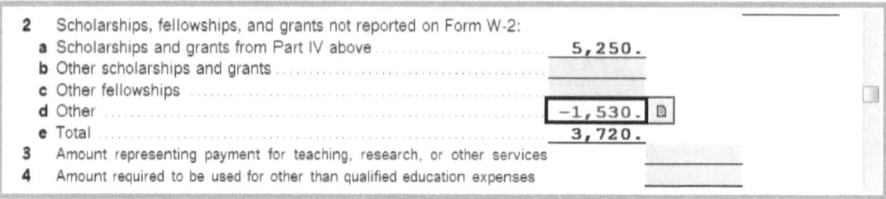

Student Information Worksheet – Scholarship Adjustment

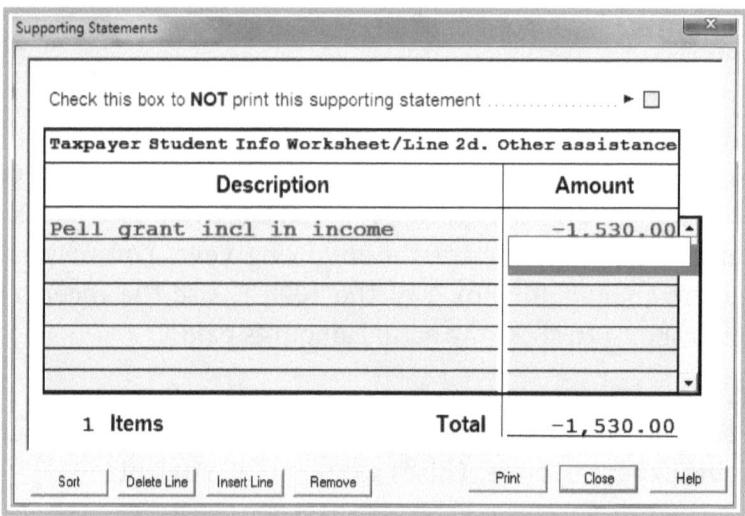

Scholarship Adjustment – Supporting Statement

You will notice that lines 3 and 4 on the Student Information worksheet can be used to enter other types of scholarships. Since there isn't an entry for elective scholarships that the taxpayer elects to include in income, it was necessary to manually adjust scholarship total and manually add the scholarships to income.

Now when you review page 2 of Form 8863, you notice that the credit has been maximized.

American Opportunity Credit

27	Adjusted qualified education expenses. **Do not enter more than $4,000**	27	4,000.
28	Subtract $2,000 from line 27. If zero or less enter -0-	28	2,000.
29	Multiply line 28 by 25% (.25)	29	500.
30	If line 28 is zero, enter the amount from line 27. Otherwise, add $2,000 to the amount on line 29 and enter the result. Skip line 31. Include the total of all amounts from all Part III, line 30 on Part 1, line 1	30	2,500.

Adjusted Form 8863

Adding scholarship income

Now that this amount of scholarships isn't offset by expenses it must be included in income. In the Income section, and under Wage, select Wages, Etc Wks (Wages, Salaries, & Tips Worksheet) and navigate to line 13. This normally does not take a manual entry so you will have to override. Right click and select override or press Ctrl-D. Note that the override will mean the field does not contain scholarship adjustments entered in line 3 or 4, so you should verify all amounts.

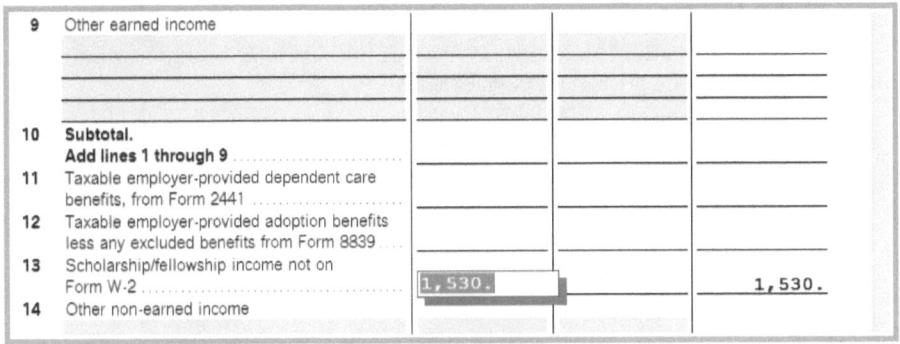

Taxable Scholarship

Note: Ideally, the 1098-T reconciliation or Student expense worksheet would have a line for this. There are currently only options to enter scholarship wages or scholarships that must be used for non-qualifying expenses. Since Pro Series is not my tax package of choice, more experienced users may have a better method.

Lacerte

Although Lacerte and Pro Series are both from Intuit, they are quite different. The procedure for Lacerte is similar to TaxWise, except that books are entered separately.

Preliminary

Using the same example as in the TaxWise and Pro Series explanations we manually calculate the net amount of qualifying expenses by subtracting tax-free scholarships from total expenses. In this example, $7,000 - $5,250 = $1,750 would be entered. In Lacerte (2013), Select the Credits tax and select Screen 38. For the field identified as qualified tuition and fees click on the box to the right of the input field to access Lacerte notes, enter the amount, and identify as Out Of Pocket expenses. These notes are the same as Detail Sheets in TaxWise and the Supporting Statements in Pro Series.

Current Year Expenses

> NOTE: Enter education expenses below not entered elsewhere.
>
> Blank=optimize, 1=force credit, 2=force tuition deduction . . . .
>
> Qualified tuition and fees (net of nontaxable benefits) . . . . `1,750` ☐
>
> Books and supplies required to be purchased from the institution . . . .
>
> Books and supplies not entered above (AOC only)

Qualified Expenses – Initial

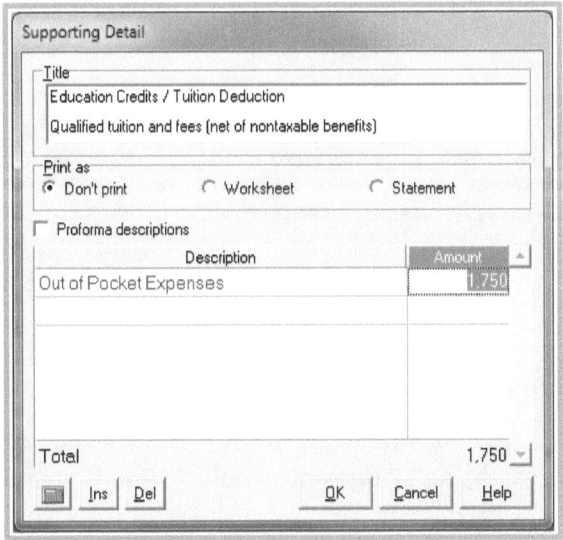

Qualified Expenses – Note

The section head of Current Year Expenses can be misleading. It suggests that the expenses are limited to the current year. Remember that the taxpayer can pay qualifying expenses in advance for the first three months of the following year.

Entering Other Expenses

Lacerte has two separate fields for entering books. The first field is for books required to be purchased from the institution. The second field is for all other books. Entries in the second field will not be qualifying expenses for the Lifetime Learning Credit. Enter the amount in the appropriate field.

Current Year Expenses

NOTE: Enter education expenses below not entered elsewhere.

Blank=optimize, 1=force credit, 2=force tuition deduction	
Qualified tuition and fees (net of nontaxable benefits)	1,750
Books and supplies required to be purchased from the institution	
Books and supplies not entered above (AOC only)	720

Qualified Expenses – Books Added

Scholarship Adjustments

Form 8863, page 2, line 27 should now show the tentative amount of qualifying expenses. If line 27 does not show $4,000 (for one student), consider possible adjustments. In this case Form 8863 shows $2,470. The difference between $2,470 and $4,000 is $1,530. Pell grants are more than $1,530 so we can include that amount in income and increase qualifying expenses.

	American Opportunity Credit		
27	Adjusted qualified education expenses (see instructions). Do not enter more than $4,000	27	2,470.
28	Subtract $2,000 from line 27. If zero or less enter -0-.	28	470.
29	Multiply line 28 by 25% (.25).	29	118.
30	If line 28 is zero, enter the amount from line 27. Otherwise, add $2,000 to the amount on line 29 and enter the result. Skip line 31. Include the total of all amounts from all Parts III, line 30 on Part I, line 1.	30	2,118.
	Lifetime Learning Credit		
31	Adjusted qualified education expenses (see instructions). Include the total of all amounts from all Parts III, line 31, on Part II, line 10	31	
BAA	FDIA3602. 12/26/13		Form **8863** (2013)

Form 8863

Add $1,530 for expenses and identify as Scholarships included in Income. This will bring the total of qualified tuition and fees to $3,280.

Current Year Expenses

NOTE: Enter education expenses below not entered elsewhere.

Blank=optimize, 1=force credit, 2=force tuition
deduction . . . .

Qualified tuition and fees (net of nontaxable
benefits) 3,280

Books and supplies required to be purchased from
the institution . . . .

Books and supplies not entered above (AOC only)   720

Qualified Expenses – Scholarships Added

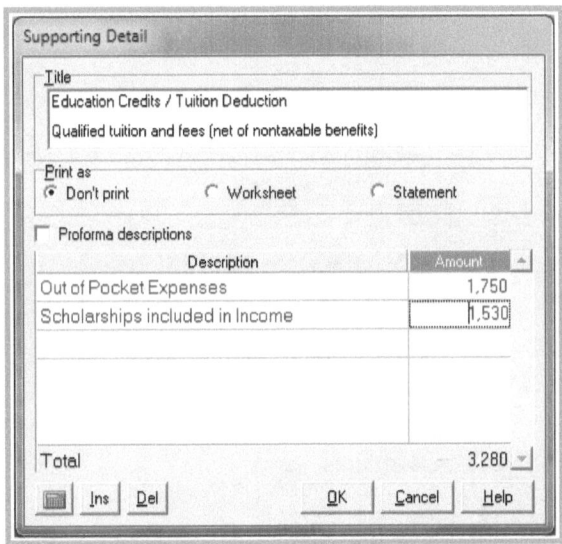

Supporting Detail

_T_itle
Education Credits / Tuition Deduction
Qualified tuition and fees (net of nontaxable benefits)

_P_rint as
⦿ Don't print   ◯ Worksheet   ◯ Statement

☐ Proforma descriptions

Description	Amount
Out of Pocket Expenses	1,750
Scholarships included in Income	1,530
Total	3,280

[📷] [_I_ns] [_D_el]   [_O_K] [_C_ancel] [_H_elp]

Qualified Expenses – Notes Adjusted

The 8863 should now show $4,000 on line 27 for qualified education expenses and calculate the potential amount of credit as $2,500.

American Opportunity Credit

27	Adjusted qualified education expenses (see instructions). **Do not enter more than $4,000**	27	4,000.
28	Subtract $2,000 from line 27. If zero or less enter -0-.	28	2,000.
29	Multiply line 28 by 25% (.25)	29	500.
30	If line 28 is zero, enter the amount from line 27. Otherwise, add $2,000 to the amount on line 29 and enter the result. Skip line 31. Include the total of all amounts from all Parts III, line 30 on Part I, line 1	30	2,500.

Lifetime Learning Credit

31	Adjusted qualified education expenses (see instructions). Include the total of all amounts from all Parts III, line 31, on Part II, line 10	31	

BAA   FDIA3602L 12/26/13   Form **8863** (2013)

Form 8863 – Adjusted

Adding Scholarship Income

Now that this amount of scholarships isn't offset by expenses it must be included in income. In Lacerte that entry is made in Screen 14.1, Miscellaneous in the Alimony and Other Income section. Identify the amount in the note as Scholarships to Increase Education Expenses.

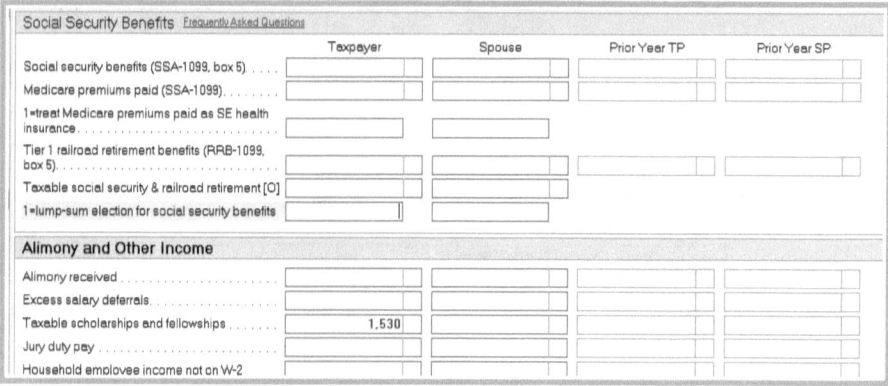

Taxable Scholarships Added to Income

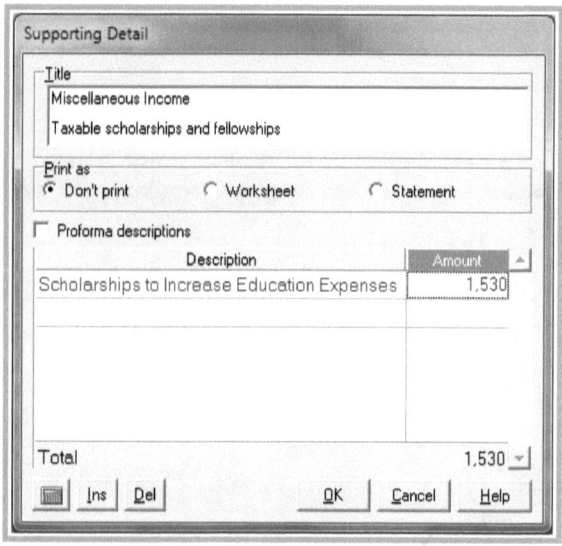

Taxable Scholarships Added – Notes

Drake (2013)

Education Credits in Drake are handled the same way as TaxWise and Lacerte, by manually calculating and entering the net amount of expenses and the amount of taxable scholarships. Double-clicking on the field allows you to attach a Detail worksheet to the input as in the former programs.

ATX (2012)

Education Credits in ATX is mostly manual as well, although the input screens for Form 8863 does have a line for American Opportunity Credit course materials. It does not provide input for scholarships though so expenses should be entered net of scholarships. ATX also does not have a calculating Detail sheet. The notes that can be added to a field are text based only.

TaxSlayer (2013)

TaxSlayer will also require the preparer to make all calculations manually without the benefit of a worksheet or detail sheet.

Others

It is crucial that the preparer knows how to calculate the relevant amounts for education credits. They will only need to know the particular software they are using, but it is to their advantage to understand all of the details. At a minimum, the preparer should prepare sample returns using the examples providing in Publication 17, and Treas. Reg. § 1.25A-5.

Documentation of the required procedures, similar to the examples in this text, will go a long way toward eliminating confusion during tax season.

Amending for Education Credits

Amending

When practitioners see clients they often like to see the prior year's return(s). That helps them to know what kind of credits and deductions they have taken in the past, or highlights a carryover for the current tax year. A bright preparer will also reverse that logic. If he discovers that the taxpayer has credits or deductions this year that were not reported on the prior year's return he can question the taxpayer about whether he qualified for credits and deductions for the prior year, and then amend those returns. At that time, they may want to review the other two prior returns as well.

Many taxpayers may be left in the dark because institutions are not required to prepare 1098-Ts when all expenses are paid for by scholarships and grants. Practitioners should question any taxpayer in school, or with children in school about the nature of their educational expenses. Locally I would advise asking about credits claimed for going to a college that limits when they provide a 1098-T.

If taking advantage of Regulation 1.25A-5 in maximizing education credits is a new revelation, amending prior year returns can multiply the benefit by a factor of four and potentially earn $10,000 in education credits. The net amount may be less if scholarships are included in income since only 40% of the credit is refundable. When filing a return in the spring semester of the student's senior year a taxpayer (student or parent) can amend returns for his freshman, sophomore, and junior year at the same time he files his senior year return. As previously mentioned, there may be years that are more beneficial than others, so planning is still a factor.

Amending returns could also be used to change prior year decisions related to education credits. If you didn't maximize the credit in one year and you can in a following year, you may want to amend. You need to be careful, however, since you could be subject to late payment penalties if you have to repay for the credit.

You can amend tax returns up to 3 years after their due date (without extensions). Thus, tax years 2011, 2012, and 2013 can all be amended before April 15 of 2015. If you do not have copies of your return, you can access your tax return information from the IRS website.

IRS transcript

The IRS makes taxpayers prior year return information available on line using transcripts. The actual return is not there but the information you will need to review or amend a return is available. Using your browser go to

http://www.irs.gov/Individuals/Get-Transcript

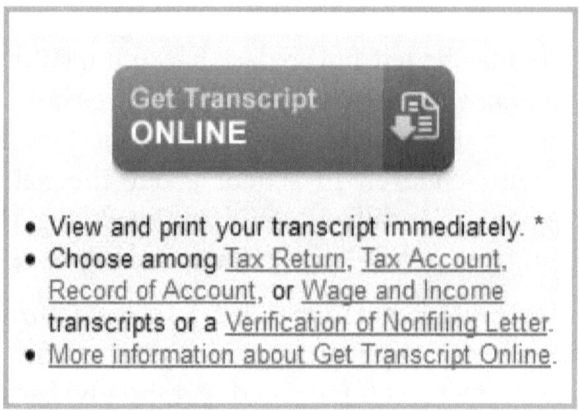

irs.gov – Get Transcript

Select Get Transcript Online

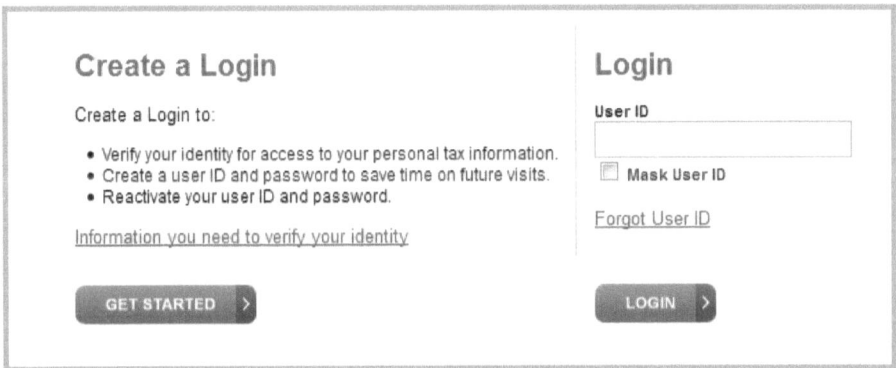

Get Transcript – Login

Log in to the site with your User ID and password (next screen). If you have not logged in before you will have to create an account. The IRS will ask several questions to verify your identity.

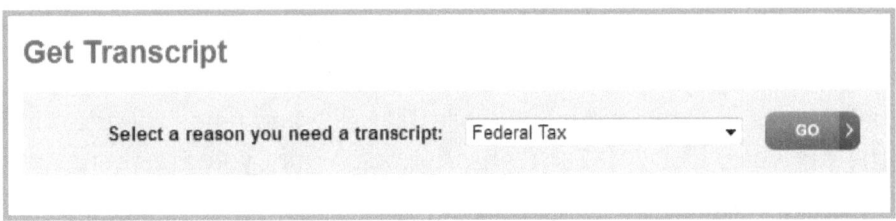

Transcript Options

Select a reason for requesting your transcript: **Federal Tax**

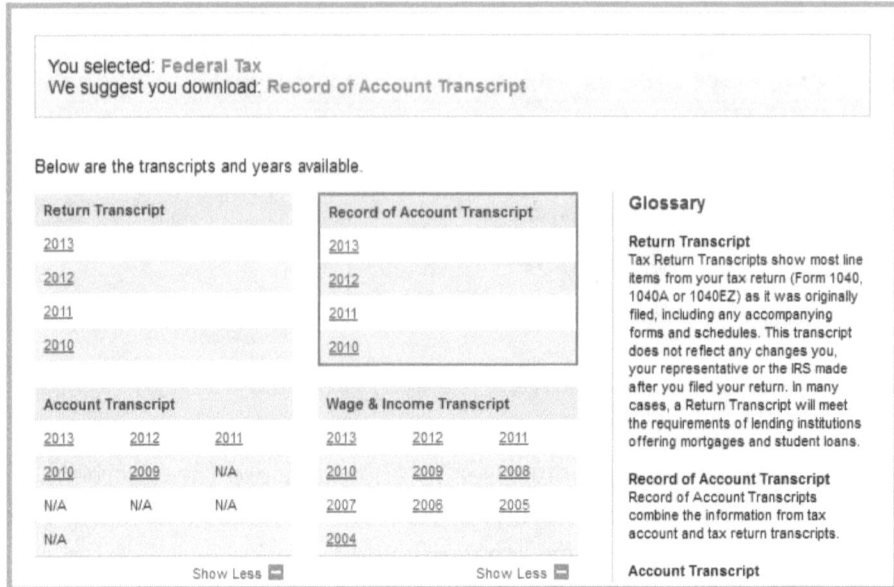

Federal Tax Transcripts

Record of Account Transcript (includes return transcript) for year

Select the tax year you want to retrieve. The tax year is the year before you file your return. Choose Save File and name the file with the tax year, like 2013TaxTranscript.pdf. While you are there, you may want to get all four years available. Print or provide the files to your preparer.

Special Issues

The reporting for Education Credits could affect a number of other areas, so a careful eye is essential. These are just a few possible side effects or concerns to watch out for.

AGI

By including scholarships in income AGI increases and tax may be owed on the scholarship amounts. The first $2,000 of expenses generates a 100% tax credit, but the second $2,000 only generates a 25% tax credit. If the marginal tax rate is above 25%, then it may be better to only include $2,000 of elective scholarships in income. The increase in AGI could also initiate phase-outs or subject the taxpayer to AMT.

AOTC Phase-out:

AOTC is subject to a phase-out. The phase-out is essentially based on percentage of income between lower and upper phase-out limits. Thus, $1000 over (based on $10,000 range) would reduce your credit by 10%.

If you happen to be put into the phase-out range by including scholarships and grants in income, re-calculate the credit omitting some or all of the scholarships to determine the most advantageous treatment. Generally, it will be most advantageous to include the first $2000 of expenses regardless of including scholarships in income. Above the first $2000, the net benefit will largely depend on your marginal tax rate and deductions.

Credit Offsets

The AOTC may be offset by other nonrefundable credits. If the total of the nonrefundable credits is more than the tax before scholarship adjustments, the taxpayer may not benefit from attempting to increase the credit. Ideally, only make adjustments up to the point that tax liability is reduced to zero. Evaluate the benefits on a case-by-case basis.

Earned Income Tax Credit

One of the characteristics of taxable scholarships is that it is not earned income for purposes of the EITC. Scholarship income is excluded from earned income in the calculation of the earned income credit, so be sure to report and treat it that way. Include SCH and the amount to the left of line 7 on 1040. Failing to tag that income in the margin as SCH could lead the IRS to believe you understated income. The IRS may make corrections to EITC and send the taxpayer an additional earned income credit which he doesn't deserve, and may have to repay. Only amounts you receive for teaching, research, or other services would be considered earned income. Those amounts are not tax-free scholarships although they can be used to pay education expenses qualifying for education credits.

Changes in EITC

Although scholarships are not earned income for EITC, they can affect it negatively. EITC is initially calculated on earned income in the EITC worksheet, but it is then calculated based on AGI. The lower credit amount is what the taxpayer receives. The net benefit of including the scholarships should always be considered.

Unfortunately, the credit percentage varies based on filing status and number of qualifying children, so maximizing the net benefit can be complicated in many cases. The EITC is based on a two sided scale with a plateau. There is a range for each type of claimant where the EITC is maximized. For example, a MFJ taxpayer with one qualifying child for EITC the credit is maximized at $3,305 for incomes between $9,700 and $17,850. Likewise, a certain credit amount can be linked to an amount of income at both extremes. For example, the same taxpayer would receive a credit of $3,000 with income of $8,800, and with income of $19,750.

One method for determining the maximum credit is to evaluate two of the three elements (education credit, taxable scholarships, EITC) to get a range of equivalent amounts, and then maximizing that with the third. In some cases it would also be necessary to compare the net benefit on two tax returns (parent and student). A comparison of claiming strategies involving scholarship inclusion and EITC is presented in the Treasury Department 4 pager on the AOTC.[17]

Support

Scholarships as support should not be a concern with current laws. If scholarships are used for qualified education expenses, they are not considered support in determining dependency (IRC §§ 152(c)(1)(D) and (f)(5)). The code here does not define the nature of the scholarships not treated as support. Also of concern in evaluating support is the fact that the refundable portion of the education credit may require the taxpayer to provide over half of their support with earned income. Refer to the qualifications flowchart for the order of qualifications.

Education Credit Fraud

The benefits associated with education credits have been a target of tax fraud. At one point the IRS was holding and examining returns with education credits more closely. In 2013, many of the problems associated with education credits were due to forms not being completed properly, either through preparer negligence or software error. Then, earlier this year the Treasury Inspector General for Tax Administration released a report claiming that billions are paid for potentially erroneous education credit claims. Some issues involve claiming AOTC for more than four years, claiming for students that are not half-time, and claiming for expenses that are not at an eligible educational institution.

None of the fraud has reportedly been related to options made available in Regulation 1.25A-5 or the elective treatment of scholarships. Instead, the cases that made their way to Tax Court had

---

17 http://www.irs.gov/pub/irs-utl/Pell%20AOTC%204%20pager.pdf

more to do with the plain language of basic qualifications such as age requirements, dependency exemptions, actual expenses[18], prepayments[19], and phase-outs. The only case I found that concerned Treas. Reg. § 1.25A-5 was a discussion of the change in a Louisiana program (TOPS) previously mentioned. Incidentally, the fact that there are so few cases that deal with the elective nature of scholarship income suggests that these regulations may be underutilized.

The TIGTA report may not be that dismal since it identified most of the credits as potentially erroneous simply because a 1098-T was not provided. A 1098-T is not required and the report does not indicate that they are aware of that. That presumption highlights one of the biggest flaws of education credit laws. Without a 1098-T the IRS does not know if a student is half-time, or if even attending. Even with a 1098-T, the IRS has no way to determine whether a credit is fraudulent without knowing all costs, payments, and options available to the taxpayer. That would require institutions to not only issue 1098-Ts for all students, but also report scholarships and grants and their treatment options, and that would only provide them with the information needed to investigate returns. The limited 1098-T reporting requirements are allowed by Treasury regulations (Treas. Reg. § 1.6050S-1(a)(2)(iii)) and not in the law (IRC § 6050S), and it appears that Congress is not willing to demand more complete reporting.

Still, the TIGTA is pressuring the IRS to lower the fraud rate for education credits, so it is imperative that taxpayers have and retain documentation to support their education credit claims. See the section on Documentation below.

---

18 Adams v Comm'r, Tax Court Summary Opinion 2013-57.
19 Jayesh B. v Comm'r, Tax Court Summary Opinion 2006-40.

Common Education Credit Errors

The IRS has a list of the most common education credit errors at http://www.eitc.irs.gov/Other-Refundable-Credits/aotcllc/errors. The following summarizes the most common mistakes taxpayers make for which a claim may be denied.

- A student that did not attend a college, university or vocational school
- Eligible education expenses were not paid or not considered as paid
- Expenses were unqualified expenses
- Credit for an eligible student for more than 4 years
- Deduction for Tuition and Fees on Form 1040, line 34 was made for the same student.

Although preparers will usually know the limitations of the AOTC, the taxpayer may not. A thorough review of the client or familiarity with the client's situation is essential to avoid these pitfalls. These are only the most common errors. Preparers should review all qualifications for each claim for the credit.

1098-T

Although the 1098-T may not be accurate or required to claim an education credit, the IRS may look at their 1098-T records to determine if a student was attending a college or university. Colleges and universities are not required to submit or provide a 1098-T to their students in many cases. If one is not on file, the taxpayer could receive a Form 886-H-AOC requesting alternate proof of attendance. The form details the information that the IRS is requesting. This is where documentation is important.

Documentation

Keep all documents that may be requested by the IRS. The taxpayer may need to provide documentation for education credits to show qualifying expenses paid, student qualifications, or information about the education program. Required documentation will be different depending on the credit or deduction claimed and the taxpayer's individual circumstances.

Receipts

Receipts for expenses are necessary to prove expenses. The student's school account records can provide much of this support. The list of expenses provided on the school account information should be detailed enough to show which expenses are qualifying expenses for the particular credit. Receipts for books purchased elsewhere will also need to be kept.

Course Descriptions and Degree Plan

Additional requirements may include a description of the courses, including what books are required for the courses, and the degree plan. Optional books are not considered qualifying expenses although they may be listed on the course syllabus along with required books for the course. Although the course syllabus typically outlines the required books, individual instructors may require different texts. That should be documented at the time. Emails or other documents from the instructor may be useful in this case.

Scholarship Terms

If the credit was increased by including scholarships and grants in income it may be necessary to document scholarship inclusion support. Just as you would document that amounts were paid, or that a scholarship was used for qualified expenses, you should document your ability to treat scholarships as taxable income. Keep some official source document that says the scholarship may be used for other than qualified expenses, i. e. room and board. Official letters from the institution or printouts from official web pages would be some examples.

Family Coordination

If scholarships were included in the income of the student to increase the parent's credit amount, that information should be maintained. This should be done even though a student's scholarship income doesn't require the student to file a tax return.

Questions

There are some questions related to education credits. Here's a few I've come up with.

Books purchased by a third party (not at institution)

The regulations say that an amount paid to the institution is considered an amount paid by the taxpayer. The taxpayer can also include expenses paid for required books and supplies even though they are not paid to the institution. But, what about amounts paid by a third party for required books purchased outside of the institution? Are those also considered paid by the taxpayer? Since the law does not specifically include that in the description, the taxpayer should assume that they do not, although IRS publications do not list that as a restriction.

Regulation Example Confusion

One of the areas where the law is unclear concerning AOTC is the wording of examples in the regulations that appear to conflict with the procedures for determining qualified expenses for the credit. Given the examples some have argued that the taxpayer must have paid expenses out of pocket, or that the taxpayer must have had non-qualifying expenses. While my opinion is that examples within the regulations are like Private Letter Rulings, in that they cover specific scenarios and do not have the power to alter the primary regulations, it is possible that the IRS or Tax Court will rule differently. My opinion is that it is not likely. Given the IRS' own promotion of Treas. Reg. § 1.25A-5, it is quite reasonable to assume that taxpayers can indeed "include [certain] scholarships in income to increase the education credit." If there is a change in procedure and processes for calculating qualifying expenses, I suspect that the IRS will provide additional guidance first.

Conservatism

Professional Conservatism is a valuable tool for protecting the liability of practitioners. While it is possible to make many arguments for their clients, it is often much safer to be conservative.

In that case, consider how the IRS might rule is such situations and how the Tax Court might rule. If the taxpayer cannot irrefutably argue the case for a particular position, it may be wiser to assume the position that the IRS can make. Actual arguments with the IRS can be costly.

A review of the Internal Revenue Manual can be invaluable in understanding the standards that IRS agents follow in examining a return, and the types of information they may request from taxpayers. The manual can be accessed at www.irs.gov/irm. Searching the manual is not a native feature of the website, but most search engines support the site: option. To search a term in the manual add site:irs.gov/irm to the end of the search string to limit the search to that website.

Amended Returns Regulations

I've often advised taxpayers that they can amend their tax returns for up to three years from the due date. The part of the IRC related to amended returns, however, is more complex and confusing than you might expect. In section IRC § 6511(b)(2)(A), for example, we can read limits on the amounts of an amended return.

(A) Limit where claim filed within 3-year period

If the claim was filed by the taxpayer during the 3-year period prescribed in subsection (a), the amount of the credit or refund shall not exceed the portion of the tax paid within the period, immediately preceding the filing of the claim, equal to 3 years plus the period of any extension of time for filing the return. If the tax was required to be paid by means of a stamp, the amount of the credit or refund shall not exceed the portion of the tax paid within the 3 years immediately preceding the filing of the claim.

A layman's reading of the code suggests that the taxpayer can't receive more refund than he paid in taxes during the look-back period (statute of limitations). One instance where this would be relevant is when the taxpayer owes taxes during one of the three years. That would make sense when referring to taxes withheld.

However, it might be argued that this section says taxpayers are not allowed refundable credits with amended returns. Court cases have dealt with the questions related to this section of the code, but they have primarily dealt with time limitations.

Concerning education credits, there is a notice, however, that alters the originally proposed regulations, which would have restricted the credits to those claimed on a timely filed return. Notice 99-32 provided that taxpayer may amend their returns to claim education credits. Likewise, sections in the Internal Revenue Manual instruct IRS staff to advise taxpayers to amend their return for such refundable credits. Section 6511 is one of many IRS code sections that need to be clarified, but it isn't one to be concerned about in relation to education credits.

Alternate Treatments

Many preparers do not take advantage of Treas. Reg. § 1.25A-5 to re-characterize scholarships and the biggest reason is that they don't know about it. However, there are others who are aware of it but who do not fully take advantage of the regulations, possibly out of fear, and add other requirements that are not a part of the regulations.

The most popular belief is that the credit is limited by the amount paid "out of pocket." Often, this belief also ignores student loans being used for expenses. Then there is the assumption that scholarship amounts must go to cover qualified expenses first, something that I would assume without knowing the law. Another treatment is to limit the amount of qualifying expenses to "own money" or the amount paid out of pocket. Tax-Aide, the volunteer service that is part of the AARP Foundation is one service that incorporates this limitation. A similar treatment is to limit the amount that can be re-characterized by the amount of non-qualifying expenses paid.

All of these treatments could also restrict the amounts to amounts paid through the institution. In these cases proponents read-into the law procedures that do not exist in the code or the text of the regulations.

Out of pocket

It's a common belief that taxpayers can only claim credits based on expenses paid out of pocket. Some IRS personnel have even said this. You can see variations of that on all kinds of websites, including tax software websites.[20] As is often the case, the information is true, but incomplete.

In some cases, the information is provided with outdated information. Many institutional websites still mention the Hope Scholarship which covers 2 years, and have not updated information on the AOTC.

One of the reasoning behind the out of pocket philosophy is that people believe that scholarships and grants are used to cover qualifying expenses before the taxpayer's payments are considered. While that is fundamental to the requirement in IRC § 25A(g)(2), that is only true for some scholarships. With many, if not most, scholarships and grants, taxpayers have a choice of what to use to pay for educational expenses.

Own Money

The reasoning for the more complicated "own money" treatment lies in the way examples are worded in the regulations and the examples in Publication 970. When the example says an amount that is re-characterized as taxable "can" be used to pay non-qualifying expenses such as room and board, their assumption is that the amount "must" be used to pay non-qualifying expenses.

Tax-Aide policy

Knowledge of Treas. Reg. Section 1.25A-5 which permits scholarship inclusion is still very limited even though it was passed more than a decade ago. But there are variations that introduce a new strain of ignorance. While the national Tax-Aide office recognizes that some

---

20   http://support.accountant.intuit.com/law-war/product=LACERTE_TAX&id=GEN68250

scholarships can be included in income to increase qualifying expenses for the AOTC, their rules are that the regulation only applies if, and to the extent, the taxpayer has paid some of their own money to the institution. They have provided a spreadsheet as a way to calculate the credit and taxable scholarships.

In the response from Tax-Aide Operations I received the following information concerning the calculations.

> *The calculator requires that there be some "own money" be in the student account - either credit card, student loan, check or other payment made by the student or on behalf of the student. If there is no "own money," there can be no education credit....*

> *SPEC headquarters is aware of this difference of opinion: that some people believe that if the tax is paid on the grant, then it is not a tax-free grant, and expenses do not need to be reduced by the amount of the grant. IRS is in negotiations with Treasury to reach a definitive decision on this question. They have promised to send a Volunteer Alert when there is the final agreement between IRS and Treasury. In the meantime, the IRS has issued final instructions for Form 8863. "Own money" is necessary to claim an education credit. The education calculator incorporates the current IRS instruction....*

> *IRS and Treasury have different interpretations of this part of the code. We asked for clarification, and SPEC has promised to issue a volunteer tax alert when there is a definitive answer. In the meantime, Tax-Aide will follow the IRS's interpretation as set forth on page 4 of the recently released 8863 instructions.*

The regulations do not mention an "own money" requirement. In fact, Example 3 in Pub 970 demonstrates that no "own money" is required to be paid for qualifying expenses. The student received a $5600 scholarship to pay for $5600 in expenses. He treated $1600 as tax-free and included the other $4000 in income so he could receive the maximum education credit. With that example it is clear that the IRS requirements do not ask how the qualifying expenses were paid. It's obvious that the expenses were paid using the scholarship money that was included in income.

Since I've already covered the argument against the "own money" alternate treatment in a blog entry, I will forego addressing the specific question in detail other than through the Literal Interpretation section presented below. Furthermore, their reference to a conflict between the IRS and the Treasury suggests that they do not understand tax law and tax administration.

Limit to Non-Qualifying Expenses

The newest argument for limiting education expense claims is limiting the expenses paid by amounts included in income to the amount of expenses paid for non-qualifying expenses.

This treatment puts the law and regulations upside down. The law limits the credit based on qualifying expenses, while this makes non-qualifying expenses a crucial element of the calculations. That condition is not present in either the law or the regulations. While incorrect, the efforts of tax preparers to limit the expenses may be considered appropriate advice to avoid tax penalties. In the case of Tax-Aide and VITA, the restrictions are safeguards to insure that inappropriate credits are not being claimed.

That argument has been so persuasive that the Pell AOTC 4 pager (now 5 pages) on Pell grants was modified to indicate allocation of Pell grants to living expenses should be limited to actual living expenses. Since that is not part of any IRS regulation or other ruling, it would not be a binding requirement per se. Practitioners can use that as a safeguard if desired though the lower-income requirements of both Pell grants and AOTC would indicate that they will not have living expenses much greater than any aid received.

Literal Interpretation

Following is an argument for the literal interpretation that I used in response to one of the alternate treatment rules.

First, the regulations generally identify qualified expenses as amounts paid for a student, from any source.

Treas. Reg. 1.25A-5[21]

> *(b) Educational expenses paid by a third party—*
>
> *(1) In general. Solely for purposes of section 25A, if a third party (someone other than the taxpayer, the taxpayer's spouse if the taxpayer is treated as married within the meaning of section 7703, or a claimed dependent) makes a payment directly to an eligible educational institution to pay for a student's qualified tuition and related expenses, the student is treated as receiving the payment from the third party and, in turn, paying the qualified tuition and related expenses to the institution.*

According to these regulations amounts paid for qualified expenses can be from any source, taxpayer, child, rich uncle, granny, and even scholarships and grants. No "own money" is required. That qualified expenses include amounts paid from scholarships and grants is further indicated by the next subsection

> *(c) Adjustment to qualified tuition and related expenses for certain excludable educational assistance—*
>
> *(1) In general. In determining the amount of an education tax credit, qualified tuition and related expenses for any academic period must be reduced by the amount of any tax-free educational assistance allocable to such period. For this purpose, tax-free educational assistance means—*
>
> *(i) A qualified scholarship that is excludable from income under section 117;*

If scholarships and grants were not included in the amount of qualified expenses paid then you would not be able to reduce those expenses by that amount.

Note: The text makes it even clearer by saying "**the student is treated as receiving the payment from the third party and, in turn, paying the qualified tuition and related expenses to the institution.**" There is no distinction based on the source. Everything

---

21 http://www.law.cornell.edu/cfr/text/26/1.25A-5

is considered paid by the student.

Second, not only does the regulation define what qualified expenses are, it prescribes this as the method of adjusting them. Given the qualified expenses paid, the taxpayer reduces them by tax-free scholarship amounts. It's a very simple process.

Third, if the taxpayer can treat a scholarship amount (Pell grants) as taxable, he can choose NOT to reduce the expenses by that amount if he includes it in income.

> *(3) Scholarships and fellowship grants. For purposes of paragraph (c) (1)(i) of this section, a scholarship or fellowship grant is treated as a qualified scholarship excludable under section 117 except to the extent—*
>
> *(i) The scholarship or fellowship grant (or any portion thereof) may be applied, by its terms, to expenses other than qualified tuition and related expenses within the meaning of section 117(b)(2) (such as room and board) and the student reports the grant (or the appropriate portion thereof) as income on the student's federal income tax return if the student is required to file a return; ...*

That is also a simple process.

In one of my examples, the student had a Pell grant of $5,250 and qualifying expenses of $7,720 and reduced them by $3,720 tax-free scholarship money to get $4,000 in adjusted qualified expenses. The remaining scholarship funds ($5,250 - $3,720 = $1,530) are included in income. My method categorizes the expenses to make it understandable but returns the same results.

IRS Tips and notices summarize this very process in numerous places, including the 8863 instructions

> *You may be able to increase the combined value of an education credit and certain educational assistance if the student includes some or all of the educational assistance in income in the year it is received.*

That shows what to do (increase credit) and how to do it (include assistance in income).

Examples given in the publications and instructions are useful in giving scenarios, but they only illustrate the regulations. They don't alter them, and they certainly don't contradict them. All of the examples in the publications and instructions can be verified with the method given in Treasury Regulation 1.25A-5.

It's important to consider the tax code and IRS regulations, which are the definitive sources for tax law. Policies and procedures solely based on what can be surmised from IRS publications and examples do not constitute tax law. While the plain language of the regulations is unmistakable, the examples and other sources are indeed more obscure, but in my initial research of this subject I found few court decisions to clarify the regulations, probably because the law and regulations are so clear.

In summary, I don't think the IRS or Tax Court is going to say, "Okay you complied with requirements, but you did not fit into any of the examples given," and I don't think the examples can show any other intent that would change the simple procedures given in the regulations.

The fact that the IRS has not argued the out-of-pocket and non-deductible scenarios in a published case is further evidence that the policies do not reflect the intent of the code and regulations, and assurance that this interpretation will not be required by the IRS.

Resolving Tax Questions

Some of these treatments indicate a fundamental lack of understanding of tax law and tax law administration which are requirements for resolving challenging tax questions. Following are a few bits of information that may help to explain tax law to other than tax professionals.

While some tax questions are not resolved until decided by Tax Court or some other decision making body, most tax questions can be resolved by researching tax law. Understanding the layers of tax law and their force goes a long way to helping resolve issues and disputes.

IRS vs Treasury

Understanding who creates and administers tax law is primary as this correspondence with Tax-Aide illustrates.

> *There is a difference of interpretation between the IRS (Form 8863 instructions) and the Treasury Department (white paper from this summer). The white paper implies that unrestricted grants can be applied to non-qualifying expenses (like room and board), made taxable on the student's tax return, and therefore all qualifying expenses (tuition and fees and books etc.) can be used toward an education credit. But, the IRS instructions for Form 8863 make it clear that if the non-qualifying expenses are paid with the scholarships or grants, then the qualifying expenses must be paid by check, credit card, loan, etc.*

The Treasury Department and the IRS are not competing departments. The Internal Revenue Service is a function of the Treasury Department. That's why throughout the Internal Revenue Code there is often a section that says something to the effect of "The Secretary may prescribe...", referring to the Secretary of the Treasury. Internal Revenue Code Section 25A(j) says concerning regulations for the education credit,

> *The Secretary may prescribe such regulations as may be necessary or appropriate to carry out this section...*

Furthermore, those regulations are appropriately called Treasury Regulations even though the IRS releases them. The IRS releases these regulations every week. They are generally released in a Treasury Directive, such as T.D. 9034[22], which covers education credits. They are released by the Internal Revenue Service and have a header that reads

DEPARTMENT OF THE TREASURY

---

22 www.irs.gov/pub/irs-regs/td9034.pdf

Internal Revenue Service

Tax Law

It's also important to understand the difference between sources of tax law. The following web site clearly describes the force of different types of information, and a section on Resolving Tax Questions explains the force of various sources of tax law.

http://www.irs.gov/Tax-Professionals/Tax-Code,-Regulations-and-Official-Guidance

In summary, the Internal Revenue Code contains the law passed or amended by Congress and the regulations are provided by the IRS as a way to enforce the Internal Revenue Code.

Together these two have the force of law. The Internal Revenue Code and Treasury Regulations are the sources cited in tax cases. There are other forms of documents, but the Internal Revenue Manual points out specifically that IRS publications do not have the force of law.

4.10.7.2.8 (01-01-2006)

IRS Publications

1 IRS Publications explain the law in plain language for taxpayers and their advisors. They typically highlight changes in the law, provide examples illustrating Service positions, and include worksheets. Publications are nonbinding on the Service and do not necessarily cover all positions for a given issue. While a good source of general information, publications should not be cited to sustain a position.[23]

That does not limit officials from making statements, creating reports, or providing advice, but outside of official functions (e.g. Chief Counsel Advice), they generally do not constitute tax law.

---

23 http://www.irs.gov/irm/part4/irm_04-010-007.html

Other Educational Incentives

Although claiming the American Opportunity Tax Credit is the primary purpose of this book, tax professionals and advisors may find this a useful launching point to mention other financial assistance programs that students/parents may not be aware of.

Often individuals only focus on qualifying for a single benefit and miss out on other benefits. Financial advisors, including preparers offering free advice should make them aware of other incentives when possible. The availability of financial aid information is fairly common knowledge to many, but it may not be so familiar for the first time student or his parent.

Timely knowledge of educational incentives is important. While the AOTC can be claimed on an amended return, other financial aid is often governed by a strict time table and educational planning needs to begin years in advance. This is particularly true for educational savings accounts. This section introduces other tax incentives for education, provides basic information on financial aid, and closes with a few words about student loans. This is just an introduction, so if any subject interests you make other inquires about the program.

Educational Savings

Using an educational savings account is one of the most popular methods of saving for college. The bonuses of these accounts are that as an investment account they often earn more money and earnings can be used tax-free for educational expenses. The two general types of savings accounts are Section 529, or Qualified Tuition Programs (QTP), and Coverdell Education Savings Accounts. Yet another savings option is to purchase certain savings bonds that can have interest excluded from income when redeemed for qualified educational expenses.

The following table compares the basic features of the two types of educational savings accounts.

Educational Savings Compared

	Section 529 plans	Coverdell Education Savings Accounts
Contributions	Non-deductible	Non-deductible
Contribution Limits	Based on an estimate of the cost of a qualified education expenses. Each state defines allowable contributions for that state's plan. In some cases, it is over $300,000 per beneficiary.	Total of $2,000 per beneficiary per year from all sources. Individual contributors are also limited by their MAGI
Phase-out limitations	None	MAGI between $190,000 and $220,000 (joint) or $95,000 and $110,000 (single)
Distributions	Excluded from income if used to paid qualified expenses	Excluded from income if used to paid qualified expenses
Qualified Expenses	Tuition, fees, books, supplies, and equipment, including room and board. Special needs	Tuition, fees, books, supplies, and equipment, including room and board. Special needs
Education Level	College	High school or college
Attendance Requirement	No restriction. Room and board is expense only if at least half-time	No restriction. For college, room and board is expense only if at least half-time
Beneficiary Limitations	May be determined by individual programs.	Contributions made before beneficiary is age 18. Distributed before beneficiary is age 30.

Federal Financial Aid	Counted as asset of the account owner. If owned by grandparent or other third-parties it is not on FAFSA.	Counted as asset of the account owner. If owned by grandparent or other third-parties it is not on FAFSA.
Investments	Restricted list of investment options depending on the program, changed only annually or under special circumstances	Owner is not restricted. Accounts can be opened at any bank and can include mutual funds, stocks. Buy/sell as often as desired.
Penalties	Withdrawn earnings not used for education subject to tax and 10% penalty	Withdrawn earnings not used for education subject to tax and 10% penalty

Section 529 Qualified Tuition Programs

Qualified Tuition Programs under Section 529 come in two flavors. Plans can be designated prepaid tuition plans or college savings plans. Prepaid tuition plans generally allow a person to purchase tuition credits or certificates to be used later by the beneficiary (IRC § 529 (b)(1)(A)(i)). Typically, such plans guarantee attendance costs in the future based on present contributions. Each state will have a different process for implementing prepaid tuition plans, although they are losing in popularity.

A section 529 college savings plan, however, allows owners to contribute to a savings/investment plan and use the proceeds for a designated beneficiary (IRC § 529 (b)(1)(A)(ii)). Even within these programs, there are often many options available.

The greatest benefit of a college savings plan is when contributions are made early, since earnings are not taxable when used for qualifying educational expenses. Starting early enables taxpayers to get the maximum amount of tax-free earnings. Additionally, since contributions are taxable, it is best to contribute when the person is in a lower tax bracket. Even when taxable, the taxes are deferred until distributed.

Where to start

Individuals can start a Section 529 plan by applying to the state directly or through a financial advisor. In many cases the individual would apply to the state in which you are a resident or that the beneficiary will be attending, but that is seldom necessary if you are getting a college savings plan since most states now support going to a college out of state. Still, that is something you will want to confirm. The Texas plan can be used at most accredited schools (vocational, undergraduate, or graduate) in the United States, and can be opened by any U. S. resident.

One benefit of getting an in-state plan is that a state tax deduction may be available. In states like Texas that do not have a state income tax, that is usually not an issue. Note that this refers to your state of residence, and some states allow a deduction for a contribution to another state's Section 529 plan. For example, as a resident of Pennsylvania, you can get a deduction for a contribution to a Texas 529 plan.

One or more eligible educational institutions also have the ability to offer Section 529 plans. In these cases, the plan must be approved and funds must be held in a qualified trust for the exclusive benefit of the designated beneficiary (IRC § 529(b)).

The website finaid.org has a list of states that offer Section 529 plans,[24] and the The National Association of State Treasurers started the College Savings Plan Network to provide general information about Section 529 plans, which links to most 529 plan websites and provides comparisons.[25]

Contributions

The minimum amount to open a Section 529 plan is generally low. In Texas, you can open a plan with $25 though there's not much benefit

---

24 http://www.finaid.org/savings/state529plans.phtml
25 http://www.collegesavings.org

unless you make regular contributions to it. A growing number of companies allow making contributions to a plan from their paycheck. When taken out of the paycheck some employers may even make additional contributions.

Although there are no dollar limits in the tax code, the limit is the "anticipated cost of a beneficiary's qualified education expenses" (IRC § 529(b)(6). In order to resolve this states limit the total amount of contributions to an account. In Texas, the current limit is $370,000. Although multiple accounts can be opened for the same beneficiary, the limits apply to the aggregate amount.

Gift taxes

One other limit that may be of concern is the gift tax limit. You can contribute $14,000 per beneficiary (70,000 for five-year contributions) before being subject to gift tax reporting. This is the amount for 2015 and it is adjusted for inflation. For most people, the gift tax itself will not be an issue. Taxpayers are allowed a lifetime limit of $5.43 million (also adjusted for inflation) in gifts which does not include the annual $14,000 that taxpayers can gift to each person. Amounts over the $14,000 per person have to be reported on a gift tax return. Gift tax rules in IRC § 529(c)(5)(B) may also apply if there is a change in beneficiary. Estate Tax issues are addressed in IRC § 529(c)(4).

Gift Contributions

Not only can taxpayers open an account for a beneficiary, third-parties can make contributions to that account if the account accepts third-party gifts. The Texas College Savings Plan accepts third-party gifts.[26] Once contributed, though, contributions can only be withdrawn by the account owner or beneficiary.

Note that gifts made through payment of tuition directly to an institution are considered qualified transfers and are not considered for gift tax purposes (IRC § 2503(e)(2)(A)).

---

26 http://www.savingforcollege.com/grandparents/answer.php?
grandparent_faq_id=6

Matching Contributions

In addition to gift contributions, matching contributions are also a possibility. Some states and some employers will match a contribution to a Section 529 plan up to a certain amount. Texas does not provide that benefit but bordering Arkansas does, as well as a handful of others.

State tax deductions

Individuals in states with an income tax may be able to take a deduction for contributions to a Section 529 plan. Since Texas does not have a state income tax, a tax credit would not apply. Not all schools, states have such a program. The website savingforcollege.com provides a list of states and their programs.[27]

Employer tax credits

In a few states employers can earn a tax credit for matching contributions to a Section 529 plan. Nevada now provides a 25% tax credit to businesses matching contributions to 529 college savings plans, up to $500 per employee. The credit is similar to an Illinois credit that began in 2009.[28]

Rollovers and Change in Beneficiary

Individuals are allowed to take a distribution and roll over to another account for the same beneficiary only once per year (IRC § 529(c)(3)(C)(iii)). Similar to IRA rollovers, the rollover must be completed within 60 days. Simple changes in beneficiary are not subject to the annual restrictions, provided the new beneficiary is a member of the old beneficiary's family (IRC § 529(c)(3)(C)(ii)). Account owners may be subject to a rollover fee.

A word about family is appropriate in the context rollovers of Section 529 accounts. Although transfers to a new beneficiary are allowed if the new beneficiary is a family member, there are restrictions on

---

27 http://www.savingforcollege.com/college_savings_201/
28 http://www.cnbc.com/2015/08/04/will-529-plans-be-the-next-hot-employee-benefit.html

when gift and estate taxes apply.

The code allows tax-free rollovers

> *(II) to the credit of another designated beneficiary under a qualified tuition program who is a member of the family of the designated beneficiary with respect to which the distribution was made (IRC § 529(c)(3)(C)(i)(II)).*

And the term "member of family" is described in IRC § 529(e)(1) and elaborated in Prop. Treas. Reg. § 1.529-1(c) and includes

> *(1) A son or daughter, or a descendant of either;*
>
> *(2) A stepson or stepdaughter;*
>
> *(3) A brother, sister, stepbrother, or stepsister;*
>
> *(4) The father or mother, or an ancestor of either;*
>
> *(5) A stepfather or stepmother;*
>
> *(6) A son or daughter of a brother or sister;*
>
> *(7) A brother or sister of the father or mother;*
>
> *(8) A son-in-law, daughter-in-law, father-in-law, mother-in-law, brother-in-law, or sister-in-law; or*
>
> *(9) The spouse of the designated beneficiary or the spouse of any individual described in paragraphs (1) through (8) of this definition*

However, the account does not escape gift and estate taxes (Chapter 11 and 12) unless the rollover is

> *(i)assigned to the same generation as (or a higher generation than) the old beneficiary (determined in accordance with section 2651), and*
>
> *(ii)a member of the family of the old beneficiary. (IRC § 529(c)(5(B)(i) and (ii).*

A review of the code in Prop. Treas. Reg. § 1.529-1 notes that

> *If the new beneficiary is assigned to a lower generation than the old beneficiary, the transfer is a taxable gift from the old beneficiary to the new beneficiary regardless of whether the new beneficiary is a member of the family of the old beneficiary.*[29]

---

29 REG-106177-97 (www.irs.gov/pub/irs-regs/10617797.pdf)

There are other scenarios where amounts can be "rolled" INTO a Section 529 account. Coverdell accounts can be rolled over to a Section 529 account although there may be restrictions on beneficiary changes. You can contribute to an account with certain types of savings bonds. There are also other requirements and forms to file to avoid taxes on the earnings.

Contributions can also be made from a Uniform Gift to Minors Act (UGMA) or Uniform Transfers to Minors (UTMA) account, but the amounts transferred are frozen for the designated beneficiary in the UGMA/UTMA account. Amounts transferred to a Section 529 account, however, must be converted to cash. Additionally, the custodian must transfer ownership of the account to the beneficiary when he reaches majority. Since earnings in a UGMA/UTMA account are subject to taxation, this may be a smart move depending on the desired investment options. Vanguard has a web tool that may assist in determining the best choice for UGMA account assets. [30]

Rolling over an IRA directly into a Section 529 plan is not an option, however distributions from an IRA are not subject to a penalty if actually used for qualified educational expenses. The amount of the distribution may also affect financial aid applications since it is then considered income to the student.

Investment Options

All Section 529 college savings plans are investment plans and have risks depending on what investment options were chosen. However, an account owner or beneficiary cannot actually direct the investment. Section 529 plans do not have the same risk as investing in a stock portfolio. Chosen investments tend to be more conservative and diversified, and account owners must choose from an array of investment options.

Age-based or Static

Two general categories of investment plans include standard (or static) plans and age-based plans. Age-based plans change over the

---

30 https://vanguard.wealthmsi.com/ugma.php

time of the plan based on the age of the beneficiary. In the early years the plans focuses on growth, involves greater risk, with a greater share of stocks while the later years focus on security with investments increasingly in bonds. Static plans do not change based on age.

Within each of these categories owners may have other options depending on their risk tolerance. Some plans may even offer guaranteed or protected plans, although they may not provide earnings near the inflation rate. Section 529 investments are generally managed by large financial companies (fund managers), and invest in large mutual funds.

Managed or Indexed (or Blended)

In addition to the different categories, different plans can have different levels of management. Some may be managed directly by a fund manager while others will rely more on index funds. Generally, fund managers that are most active in managing an account can select investments that will generate more earnings and involve greater risk, however they will charge higher fees. Index funds depend on a common index such as the S&P 500 Index or the Vanguard Total Stock Market Index. They often have lower fees, but often have lower earnings and lower risk.

Texas has a wide array of plans to choose from, although they do not have any that are fully managed. Instead, they have either blended (active and index investments) or strictly index investments. Within both blended and index funds, owners can also select age-based or static. In both blended and index funds, later years of an age-based plan include investments in money market accounts. People who don't want to manage their fund will often select one of the age-based plans and leave it alone.

Fees

There are a number of fees associated with Section 529 accounts, including program management and maintenance charges, and underlying investment fees. Investment fees are the amounts that often represent management of the fund. For actively managed funds, these will be higher than for index funds.

In some cases, there may be adviser fees. Adviser fees only apply to plans purchased through a financial advisor or other broker. Adviser fees are generally either based on based on account balances, purchases, sales, or in some cases may be fixed dollar amounts.

If you already have a financial planner he may offer 529 plans as part of a package of services. Even your insurance agent may propose to help with educational savings plans. Some states are direct-sold only and do not sell Section 529 plans through financial advisors. On the other hand, some states will even waive account fees for certain accounts.

Your choice of a plan should consider the impact of fees on the net earnings of the account. In some cases the extra fee may be money well spent. The collegesavings.org comparisons page include a range of fees expected for different states. Texas currently estimates total fees to be 0.60% to 1.00% per year.

Texas

Texas, where everything is bigger, is one of the states that offers both types of plans. In fact, Texas has two each of tuition prepaid plans and college savings plans.[31]

Two different prepaid plans
- Texas Guaranteed Tuition Plan (closed to new enrollees)
- Texas Tuition Promise Fund

Two kinds of college savings plans
- Texas College Savings Plan – administered by the state of Texas, offers various investment portfolios.
- LoneStar 529 – access to a financial advisor, additional fees apply.

Not only are there two kinds of college savings plans, Texas has 20

---

31 https://www.texastuitionpromisefund.com/content/explore-my-options/saving-for-college-in-texas

investment options in the Texas College Savings Plan, including age-based and static plans.

Earnings and Distributions

The primary benefit of a college savings plan is that earnings are not taxable. Money withdrawn from Section 529 accounts are tax-free when used for educational expenses. Since contributions are after-tax, only earnings escape taxation. Withdrawals that are not used for qualified expense will be subject to taxes and penalties on the earnings. If a state tax deduction was previously received for making contributions, that deduction could also be recaptured and state penalties could be imposed on non-qualified distributions.

It is important to note that the potential taxability of distributions is generally on the beneficiary. The code defines taxable distributions in regard to the distributee, but notes that if the beneficiary benefits from the distribution it is considered distributed to the beneficiary (IRC § 529(c)(3)(B)(iv)). This treatment generally results in a lower (child's) tax bracket, if any amounts are taxable. That situation could result from scholarships or other assistance received for educational assistance, or claiming a deduction or tax credit. Of course, if the owner withdraws funds for personal use, they are taxable to him.

Keep in mind that unlike Section 530 Coverdell plans, there is no beneficiary age limit on contributions or distributions. An individual can use a Section 529 account designating himself or a spouse as the beneficiary. This is a special situation, however, since contributions cannot be considered completed gifts in that case. Obvious changes in circumstances, such as a change in beneficiary, will be treated according to principles of the tax code and regulations.[32]

Distributions and Support

One often overlooked aspect of distributions is how it could affect support in regards to dependency exemptions. This issue relates not only to Section 529 distributions but to all sources of income of the

---

32 Announcement 2008-17, 2008-9 I.R.B. II (D) para. 2
    (http://www.irs.gov/irb/2008-09_IRB/ar17.html)

student.[33] In order to qualify as a dependent a student cannot have provided more than half of his own support (IRC § 152(c)(1)(D)). Scholarships do not count as support (IRC § 152(f)(5)(B)).

One way to alleviate the issue is to control the amount of distributions and to time distributions. In order to escape taxation on earnings used for educational expenses, distributions must be made in the tax year or by March 31 of the following year[34], but they are taxable income in the year received. By delaying an appropriate amount until the following year, it may be possible to resolve support issues to the taxpayer's advantage.

Even though the account is an asset of the account owner, the amounts distributed may be considered amounts provided by the student for his own support. Although the issue may not be specifically addressed by the IRS, Treas. Reg. § 1.152-1(a)(2)(ii) supports this same concept in other areas.[35] For example, ownership and expenses related to an automobile used by the student may or may not be considered support depending on a number of factors. Another issue related to support is the obligation for student loan debt.

In some cases the taxpayer may want to allow the student to claim his own exemption, but diligence is required in this. Including distributions in the student's income to qualify the student for AOTC may not work as desired because the refundable portion requires the child to provide his support with *earned* income. Furthermore, parents are more likely to benefit from the non-refundable portion of the AOTC.

Distributions and Financial Aid

One other concern about distributions is that amounts distributed are considered income to the beneficiary and could affect future eligibility for financial aid. Timing will also be important in this

---

33 http://www.journalofaccountancy.com/issues/2012/mar/20114558.html
34 Announcement 2008-17, 2008-9 I.R.B. III (B)
35 http://www.thetaxadviser.com/issues/2010/aug/nichols-aug-2010.html

context. Distributions could be delayed until after financial aid need is calculated.

In a prepaid tuition plan, the concept of earnings is generally irrelevant, since in this plan the person is buying education instead of saving for education.

Reporting

Taxpayers are not required to report non-taxable distributions on their tax return. If part of a distribution is not used to pay qualified educational expenses, then that amount may need to be reported.

Form 1099-Q

Form 1099-Q issued to the beneficiary provides the amount of the distribution, basis, and earnings on which to calculate tax liability. If part of the distribution is subject to tax, Form 5329 is used to calculate and report the taxable amount and penalties if applicable.

Caveats

The rules governing Section 529 plans are frequently presented on-line, but in some cases they are generalized and either ignore certain restrictions in the law or abbreviate the requirements. Sometimes it is easy to overlook some important aspect of the plan or how it relates to other elements. Following are some things to watch out for.

Section 529 Plan Ownership

The foregoing discussion covers the taxable aspects of Section 529 related to income taxes, but there are other tax effects that may need to be considered. Federal estate and gift tax issues are specifically covered in general in the code, but account owners should be cognizant of the liability for state taxes as well as how accounts affect both federal and state financial aid qualifications. State taxes need to be examined based on the individual state. Generally, a parent-owned 529 Plan is reported as a parent asset on the FAFSA. If owned by grandparent, it is not included in FAFSA.

Prepaid Tuition Watch

The are some elements to prepaid tuition plans that need to be carefully examined. When planning a prepaid tuition plan, be careful to consider what expenses will be paid through the plan, and what expenses won't be covered. Determine if the plan pays for tuition or tuition and fees.

Although tuition is constantly rising, educational expenses also increase for required fees. These fees are also a big part of attendance and cannot be avoided. Some of these fees are included in the amounts covered by the plan. However, additional fees that are often not covered include equipment, computer access, required fees that are course-specific, or program fees related to a course of study. You may want to make plans for items not covered in a prepaid tuition plan.

Investment Control

Although funds in a Section 529 plan are invested, the account does not have direct or indirect control over the account, other than selecting a predefined investment option (IRC § 529(b)(4)).

> No investment direction
>
> A program shall not be treated as a qualified tuition program unless it provides that any contributor to, or designated beneficiary under, such program may not directly or indirectly direct the investment of any contributions to the program (or any earnings thereon).

While directing the investment is not allowed to either contributor or beneficiaries, programs do allow contributors to annually select among investment options made available by the individual state. The annual election was provided in IRS Notice 2001-55[36] and subjects the program to various limitations to disallow owners a means of directing the plan assets.

Note: In 2009, IRS Notice 2009-1 did provide a one-time rule that allowed a change in the investment strategy selected for a Section

---

36 www.irs.gov/pub/irs-drop/n-01-55.pdf

529 account twice per calendar year in 2009.[37]

Amount to Save

It is common to see that contributions are virtually unlimited in a Section 529 plan. In fact, the law restricts the amount (IRC § 529(b) (6)).

> *Prohibition on excess contributions*
>
> *A program shall not be treated as a qualified tuition program unless it provides adequate safeguards to prevent contributions on behalf of a designated beneficiary in excess of those necessary to provide for the qualified higher education expenses of the beneficiary.*

Expenses and the Half-Time Requirement

A common reading of this benefit is that amounts can be used for qualifying expenses of a student attending half-time. It is important to distinguish between different educational expenses, since they are covered in two separate paragraphs. In general, qualified expenses (no half-time requirement) are tax-free if paid from Section 529 accounts (IRC § 529(e)(3)(A)). In addition, room and board expenses can be paid tax-free from Section 529 accounts, if the student is at least half-time (IRC § 529(e)(3)(B)).

Also, room and board does not have to be in the institution, but it is limited to the allowance for room and board by the institution, or actual on-campus room and board (IRC § 529(e)(3)(B)(2)). Prop. Treas. Reg. § 1.529-1(c) limits the amount of room and board for students staying at home to $1,500 per academic year. For others the limit is $2,500 per academic year.

Also compare the half-time requirement with the AOTC qualifications. Remember that the AOTC does require a student to be at least half-time to claim any expenses.

Coverdell (Section 530)

A Coverdell Education Savings Account is similar to a Section 529 account and shares some of the same sections of tax code. However,

---

37 http://www.accountingtoday.com/ato_issues/2009_3/30659-1.html

it is also very different. With a Coverdell Education Savings Account, up to $2,000 (subject to phase-outs) can be contributed each year for each student's educational expenses. Contributions are non-deductible but they grow tax-free until distributed. Earnings are tax-free for qualified expenses.

There is a phase-out for Coverdell accounts when MAGI is between $95,000 ($190,000 joint) and $110,000 ($220,000 joint), with individuals over $110,000 ($220,000 joint) disqualified from contributing to a Coverdell during the tax year. There is a 6% excise tax on contributions exceeding the allowed contributions. Contributions are also not allowed after the beneficiary is age 18. Expenses paid from a Coverdell account can be applied to elementary, secondary or college expenses.

Unlike Section 529 programs which individual states often oversee, a Coverdell ESA is a trust or custodial account. An individual can start a Coverdell account at banks, brokerages, and other IRS-approved entities that meet the requirements established in the tax code. The beneficiary is considered the owner of the account, although it is controlled by a "responsible individual" as custodian. The custodian is also not restricted in the way the funds are invested.

For a Coverdell ESA, qualifying expenses are defined differently for elementary and secondary, and for higher education. Qualifying expenses for elementary and secondary education are expanded to include room and board, transportation, uniforms, and even computers and internet service if used by the beneficiary and family (IRC § 530(b)(3)).

Qualifying Expenses for higher education are the same as those described for Section 529 plans, and include room and board if at least half-time. The code section that describes higher education expenses (IRC § 530(b)(2)) refers to IRC § 529(e)(3) and also allows payments from Coverdell accounts to a Section 529 account. Contributions from a Coverdell account to a Section 529 are considered qualified educational expenses.

As mentioned elsewhere, qualifying expenses must be adjusted for scholarships, deductions, and credits allowed. Taxpayers will often want to pay taxes on the distribution and claim the amounts on a tax credit such as the AOTC (IRC § 530(d)(2)(C)). The amount of a distribution that equals scholarships or other adjusted expenses is then taxable but can be excluded from the 10% penalty for non-qualifying expenses (IRC § 530(d)(4)(B)).

With the exception of age limitations of new beneficiaries, rollovers follow the same rules as Section 529 accounts. Amounts in a Coverdell ESA must be distributed within 30 days after the beneficiary is age 30, or if death occurs. There are no age limitations for special needs beneficiaries.

Savings Bonds

The Treasury Department has an education savings bond program where interest from Treasury bonds can be excluded from income if used for educational expenses. Savings bonds must be Series EE or Series I U. S. Treasury bonds issued to the taxpayer after 1989 and may include the dependent student as the beneficiary. The bond's issue date (normally the 1st day of a month) must be after the taxpayer's 24th birthday (IRC § 135(c)).

Interest can be excluded for educational expenses at a qualifying educational institution, if redeemed during the same tax year. Neither room and board or books are qualifying expenses. Amounts not used for qualifying educational expenses are taxable and are pro-rated. Qualifying expenses include contributions to a Section 529 or Coverdell account (IRC § 135(c)(2)(C)).

There is a phase-out for the interest deduction based on MAGI which includes the interest before exclusion as well as other income items. The phase-out is adjusted for inflation and is between $76,000 ($113,950 joint) and $91,000 ($143,950 joint).[38] The exclusion is not available to taxpayers filing separately (IRC § 135(b)(2) and (d)(3)).

---

38 http://www.irs.gov/pub/irs-pdf/f8815.pdf

UTMA

Though not technically an educational incentive, all states have a law that allows parents to set aside amounts for their children in an irrevocable trust. Uniform Transfers to Minors Act (UTMA) and its predecessor the Uniform Gifts to Minors Act (UGMA) allow individuals to set up an account for minors and transfer funds or property into it. This act enables them to set up a trust account without an attorney, and contribute property (including securities) to it for a minor child. The UTMA account is a taxable account so there is little tax incentive in it.

The initial amounts earned are taxed to the child under age 19, but amounts above $2,000 may be taxed at the parents rate (IRC § 1(g)). Other rules apply and there are some exceptions to the general rule. The value of a UTMA account also adversely affect financial aid eligibility. Amounts in a UTMA, however, can be contributed to open a custodial Section 529 account and enjoy both the exclusion of future earnings from taxation and a gentler treatment in regards to financial aid eligibility.

Although the theory of the law is that the amounts in such accounts are considered property of the minor, and a change in beneficiary is forbidden, the IRS has anticipated issues related to UTMA account and indicates that a change in beneficiary will be considered a taxable distribution and subsequent contribution to a new account.[39]

IRAs

Individual Retirement Accounts (IRAs) are not typically thought of as a means of educational savings, but there is an exception that applies to distributions from an IRA for educational expenses.

Though not specifically an educational account, currently amounts in an Individual Retirement Account (IRA) can be withdrawn and used for educational purposes without penalty (IRC § 72(t)(2)(E)). Taxpayers will still have to pay tax on distributions of an early

---

39 Announcement 2008-17, 2008-9 I.R.B. II (D) para 6 (http://www.irs.gov/irb/2008-09_IRB/ar17.html)

withdrawal, but the 10% penalty does not apply if the distributions are used for qualified educational expenses.

Traditional IRAs are pre-tax dollars that must be included in income when distributed. If distributed prior to retirement for certain needs, including qualifying educational expenses, they avoid early distribution penalties.

Roth IRAs are after-tax and distributions from contributions are not taxed. Earnings are taxable if withdrawn before age 59½ but are not subject to a 10% early withdrawal penalty if used for qualified educational expenses. Roth IRAs also require that contributions be held for at least 5 years (IRC § 408A(d)(3)(F)(i)(II) and Treas. Reg. § 1.408A-6(b)). Contributions to a Roth IRA can be withdrawn without taxation (Treas. Reg. § 1.408A-6(b)).

Note that traditional IRAs can have both deductible or non-deductible contributions. Deductible contributions are taxed in full at ordinary rates. If not deducted, only earnings are taxed when withdrawn. After age 59½ (and 5 tax years after opening a Roth IRA), all withdrawals are tax-free.

Choosing between IRA and educational savings

A commonly heard concern is the decision between saving for retirement and saving for education. Because an IRA is more versatile people may want to consider an educational account only after making the maximum amount of IRA contributions. Unlike IRAs, contributions to a 529 or Coverdell, are locked in and can only be used for educational expenses. Also payments from a Roth IRA will generally not be considered as income to the student, whereas Section 529 accounts may affect income for financial aid determination. The interaction of these accounts and financial aid should be investigated carefully.

IRAs have the added benefit of qualifying for the current Retirement Savings Credit when contributions are made. One other benefit of an IRA is the ability to manage the account and invest the funds any way you want. After you have set up a Section 529 plan, neither the contributor or a beneficiary is allowed to direct the investments in the program (IRC § 529 (b)(4)).

There are some ways in which Section 529 accounts are better. For one, minimum contributions to start a 529 are generally lower than that of an IRA. Many fund companies require $2,500 per year to start an IRA (although the myRA will be an option when it becomes available). Before making a plan, make a thorough analysis of the benefits, risks, and potential for each person's circumstances and the available resources at the time. It's also possible that distributions could occur at a time that the taxpayer does not have any taxable consequences.

Employer-Provided Educational Assistance

There are two key opportunities by which employers can assist employees with their education. The first is a Section 127 employer-provided educational assistance program. A Section 127 program allows the employer to pay the costs of education of an employee and exclude that from the employees paycheck. The main benefit of this is that the employee and employer are both free from having to pay employment taxes on the amount.

A section 127 plan must be a qualified program for the exclusive benefit of an employer's employees and the amount of the exclusion is limited to $5,250. The program must be written and meet IRS requirements.

Some of the requirements include

- The program must not be discriminatory in favor of employees that are highly compensated. For this purpose the IRS defines highly compensated in part as a greater than 5% owner or an employee earning greater than $80,000 (IRC §§ 127(b)(2), 414(q)(1)).

- The company must also make information about the program and its terms available to eligible employees (IRC § 127(b)(6)).

- The program must not make alternate compensation

available to employee not using the program (IRC § 127(b)(4)).

- The expenses covered by this program include tuition, fees, and course materials required. Not included in the expenses are meals, lodging, transportation or any tools or supplies that will be retained by the employee following the training (IRC § 127(c)(1)). Following EGTRRA (2001), the education provided can be for undergraduate as well as graduate studies. [40]

The benefit of employer-provided assistance under Section 127 is that the employment does not have to be work-related. Additionally the benefit can be provided by a self-employed person as defined in IRC § 401(c)(1), part of which requires earned income from a trade or business. Of course the expenses can not be for education involving sports, games, or hobbies. This benefit does not allow the employee to take any deduction or credit for the expenses (IRC § 127(c)(7)).

Employers can also provide educational support as fringe benefits under IRC § 132(d). This benefit also excludes amounts of educational expenses but the expenses must otherwise be allowable as expenses under IRC § 162 or IRC § 167, that is, it must qualify as a business expense.

A third type of assistance that may be possible from an employer is a scholarship or grant. Scholarships and grants, regardless of the source are generally non-taxable if used for qualifying educational expenses. Tax-free amounts do not include room and board, transportation, or other personal expenses.

Some types of scholarships and grants can be included in income to increase qualifying educational expenses and tax credits. The different types of scholarships and grants were covered in the Regulations chapter. Scholarships and grants that are provided under the condition that the recipient perform some service are taxable income, normally reported on a W-2. This includes teaching, research, or other services.

---

40 http://www.gpo.gov/fdsys/pkg/PLAW-107publ16/html/PLAW-107publ16.htm

Financial Aid

At the undergraduate level there is a wide variety of programs that aid students financially. Many times colleges will point these out to students inquiring about financial aid. Sometimes individual incentive is required. Most schools provide or coordinate several types of financial aid, including federal and state grants, scholarships, work study, tuition reductions, and student loans. A few types of financial aid are possible outside of the school, but must often be coordinated with the school. Most require an application process through the school.

Applying for financial aid

Schools will assist students with their financial aid packages but it is ultimately up to the student to complete the required applications.

FAFSA

The first step in actually applying for federal financial aid will be to complete the Free Application for Federal Student Aid (FAFSA) at https://fafsa.ed.gov/. All federal educational assistance is dependent on information in the FAFSA. While it is a lengthy application, it is generally a one-time application which is easy to update.

FAFSA information is found on a separate website of the federal government titled Federal Student Aid at studentaid.ed.gov/sa/. Much related information is also available on that site, including common questions and answers on various topics. It will be worth studying this site before sending students off to their studies. It even includes a FAFSA4caster[41] that helps you to estimate your EFC.

The FAFSA is generally created on-line and consequently immediately submitted, but there is also a download version.[42] You may want to get that copy and use it to gather the information you will need for the on-line application.

---

41 https://fafsa.ed.gov/FAFSA/app/f4cForm
42 https://fafsa.ed.gov/fotw1516/pdf/PdfFafsa15-16.pdf.

Maximizing financial aid.

Previewing the application will also show where adjustments may need to be made to enhance the chances of receiving financial aid. It doesn't make much sense to lower your income to afford financial aid, but a few arrangements and smart timing can be important to maximizing your opportunities.

Knowing where you stand on a FAFSA is invaluable. You don't have to just apply and hope. Among other things, the FAFSA calculates your expected financial contribution (EFC), or how much you can be expected to afford. Resources are available to allow you to calculate EFC[43] and estimate aid, if it is available to the school. If it's not what you expected, you may be able to make some adjustments to improve your chances. It might also be better to figure out your FAFSA before deciding where to go to school.

Based on the school chosen, the FAFSA calculates the cost of attendance (COA). Your possible financial aid is theoretically the difference between COA and EFC.[44] As the amount of your anticipated costs increase your available aid may increase. In other words, you may be able to afford a better school with the same out-of-pocket expenses.

When planning for FAFSA note that the process changes for the 2017-2018 school year. President Obama issued an order that changes the process to use prior-prior-year income. This means the current 2015 tax year will count for both the 2016/2017 school year (old rule) and the 2017/2018 school year (new rule). [45]

The two items that are weighted most heavily in FAFSA are income (AGI on a tax return) and assets available. Since much of the affordability analysis depends on the AGI of the student (and parents

---

43 http://ifap.ed.gov/efcformulaguide/attachments/090214EFCFormulaGuid e1516.pdf
44 https://studentaid.ed.gov/sa/fafsa/next-steps/how-calculated
45 https://www.kitces.com/blog/amended-fafsa-rules-to-allow-prior-prior-year-ppy-income-data-when-qualifying-for-financial-aid/

if applicable), it would be wise to lower that amount as much as possible. Taking above the line deductions such as IRA or 401(k) contributions is one way to do that. Claiming any moving expenses is also beneficial.

Lowering the child's assets is another way to improve financial aid chances, but don't do it by cashing them in. As previously mentioned, transferring UTMA amounts (considered a student's asset) into a Section 529 account may increase the student's chances of being eligible for financial aid, or the amount of the aid. Avoid getting distributions from that account until the FAFSA has been submitted since that would then be counted as income.

Assets are also a conditional element since their consideration depends on the applicant's age. As a result, older (non-traditional) students may have an easier time to get approved. In some other cases, assets are totally ignored in the calculation. Furthermore, certain rules may generate an automatic EFC of zero, maximizing the amount of aid the student is qualified for.

The most important thing may be the timing. Apply with FAFSA in a year when prior year income (AGI) is lowest. Since part of the consideration of FAFSA is parental support, some students may be better off to wait until they are on their own and can apply as an independent student and avoid parental additions to their EFC.

Be responsible

Remember that aid comes from tax dollars. The more that is spent, the more the government will have to bring back in, or save by cutting other programs. It also doesn't make much sense to lower your income to afford financial aid.

Vital Records

In order to complete the FAFSA you will need to have filed your tax return for the most recent year. If you have filed but do not have a copy of your return you can request a copy or transcript from the IRS. See the IRS transcript guide on page 112.

Note that you may not need a return or transcript. There is a tool being developed that may be used to import relevant information from the tax return into the application. This will be most functional when the application begins depending on prior-prior-year returns.

You may also need other vital records to complete the FAFSA or the college's application forms. If you don't have all of your vital records you may be able to get them from the appropriate government entity. There is a helpful site for vital records at

https://www.usa.gov/replace-vital-documents

Deadlines

When applying for financial aid it is crucial that you consider all of the deadlines. FAFSA has deadlines for submitting the application, the states will have deadlines for state assistance, and the school will have their own deadlines for admission to the school, program admission, and local scholarships.

In addition to considering the deadlines, register as early as possible in order to get the classes you need. In many programs at smaller schools, classes are rotated and many classes will have prerequisites. Missing one class could mean a year wait. Even if you have not received aid, registration may keep your place in line.

Appeals and Exceptions

Occasionally individuals do not meet the strict requirements for financial aid but may have circumstances that could meet an exception or deserve reconsideration. For example, loss of employment that was shown on a previous tax return and no expectation of return to work, or other changes in the amount of resources that will be available are some things that may be considered.

The UT Tyler website has various forms for requesting reconsideration. Search the websites of other colleges, or contact the college offices personally to see if an exception or reconsideration might be available to you.

Federal Grants

Much of the available financial aid is provided in the form of federal grants. See the following website for a discussion of some federal grants that are available at the time of application.

https://studentaid.ed.gov/sa/types/grants-scholarships

Pell grants

The Pell grant is the most popular and readily available form of financial aid for low-income students and families. As a grant, the student is not responsible for repayment of the amounts received if conditions are met. Withdrawing from classes could subject you to repayment. Academic performance may be required in order to continue receiving assistance. The total Pell grant reward has a lifetime limit on the number of college hours it is available for, which will depend on the hours required in the program.

FSEOG

A Federal Supplemental Educational Opportunity Grant (FSEOG) is a grant for undergraduate students with exceptional financial need. If the school participates in this program, students could receive FSEOG funds before they receive the Pell grant. Unlike the Pell grant the FSEOG is limited on a school basis, so there is no guarantee that the grant will be awarded to all eligible students. Applying early will improve the chances of receiving the FSEOG and similar grants.

TEACH

As the title suggests, the TEACH grant is provided to prospective teachers, and it requires students to sign an agreement and be in a TEACH-grant program at the school. Although this is a federal program, it is administered by each individual school and must meet their requirements.

One requirement is that the recipient may have to sign an agreement to serve. Failing to meet the agreement conditions will mean the grant becomes a student loan instead. The most recent agreement requirements are that the student must agree to serve as a full-time teacher for at least four years after completing or ending the TEACH grant program. The school must be a low-income school and in a high-need field. Other requirements will need to be met and some exceptions may be available.

Special Grants

Some grants are focused on special needs or interests. One of the special grants available from the federal government is the Fulbright grant an international exchange program. It is administered by the State Department's Bureau of Educational and Cultural Affairs (ECA). More information is available at http://eca.state.gov/fulbright.

Exceptions

Like many programs, there are allowances and exceptions for unusual circumstances, so reviewing the options is important. For example, Pell grants are only available for a certain number of hours. If the final semester requires you to go over that amount, they may approve of the plan. You may also be able to re-apply for certain types of aid based on changes in expected income that is not reflected in the latest FAFSA.

College Scholarships and Grants

Scholarships and grants available at colleges include several kinds. While academic and sports based scholarships are popular, other scholarships are available. Academic scholarships are often available to entering and continuing students. Others are targeted toward a particular occupation or category of occupation, such as nursing, accounting, or science in general.

Many scholarships, including academic scholarships, are need-based. Some colleges have a list of endowed scholarships that individual donors sponsor for needy students.

Taxability

Scholarships can be taxable. Although scholarships are thought to be tax-free, if the amounts received were not spent for qualified expenses, or exceed qualified expenses, they are taxable income.

Some scholarships can be included in income in order to qualify for education credits. See the initial chapters on the American Opportunity Tax Credit (AOTC) for more information about the AOTC and types of scholarships.

Although this text focuses on college level education, scholarships and grants are also tax-free if used for qualified elementary or secondary school expenses. The school must maintain a faculty and a body of regularly enrolled students in attendance (IRC §§ 117 (b), 170(b)(1)(A)(ii)).

Work Study

Many colleges provide assistance through work study programs. Work study programs may or may not depend on financial need, depending on the school or the department. Some work study is paid by grant, and to qualify you have to have need. Work study is also available outside of the college.

Students should keep in mind that only limited cases allow employers to have non-paid work study. This includes internships in particular. While employers sometimes look at students as cheap or free labor, there are federal restrictions on the use of work study in the U. S. Work study income is taxable income, though educational expenses paid from work study income may qualify for credits or deductions.

Qualified Tuition Reduction

In addition to employer-provided educational assistance, academic institutions can offer another form of assistance tax-free. These are generally defined on a state or college level and usually include free tuition to employees or family members. The IRS allows these tuition reductions in IRC § 117(d). Qualified Tuition Reductions (QTRs) can only be offered by schools and are not subject to any dollar limit. However, QTRs generally only cover tuition.

Texas provides such a program of tuition waivers subject to institutional allowances. Elements of the program are discussed in Texas code Chapter 54, Subchapter D. The website lists many of the available waivers at

http://www.collegeforalltexans.com/apps/financialaid/tofa.cfm
?Kind=E .

In addition to waivers benefiting employees, there are waivers (or tuition reductions) for a wide range of individuals, including high-ranking high school seniors, veterans, and senior citizens.

Individual institutions will likely provide information on which waivers they permit. The UT Tyler web site listing their waivers is at http://www.uttyler.edu/financialaid/exemp_waivers.php

Federal Training Programs
There are other federal programs that provide incentives to workers to learn a new trade including the Trade Adjustment Assistance (TAA)[46] and the Workforce Innovation and Opportunity Act (WIOA)[47]. Both of these programs are targeted, meaning they focus on a particular type of employee, or they focus on training for a specific business or trade.

Both are generally administered by a state agency, such as the state workforce commission. They are often limited to developing skills in a trade through a short-term training programs leading to certificates rather than degrees but sometimes they allow recipients to begin an educational program that meets a particular occupational need of the area.

Student Loans

For families or students who do not have money for all costs of education, student loans are usually available. There are several different types of loans depending on financial aid, source, and funding. The most beneficial type of loan is one that is subsidized, that is, the government pays part of the cost of the loan. Generally the interest rate is lower and some of the interest may be paid during a deferral period, such as while attending school. Stafford loans are

---

46 http://www.doleta.gov/tradeact/
47 http://www.doleta.gov/wioa/

subsidized.

Unsubsidized loans are also available from the federal government, and students can also make loans at private banks. Student loans can often meet the needs for living expenses that won't usually be covered by scholarships and grants.

One other benefit of federal student loans is that various payment plans may be available, including an income based repayment plan. One issue related to student loans, however, is that if they are made by the student they are considered support provided by the student in determining dependency. Repayment obligations, then, should be considered carefully.

Student Loan Interest Deduction

There is little incentive in getting a student loan simply because you are expected to repay it, with interest. But it may enable one to complete a degree program that might otherwise be impossible. One small consolation is that interest on a student loan can be deducted from income. The deduction is available for student loans for the taxpayer, spouse, or a dependent and is limited to $2.500 a year. At the 15% tax bracket that is only a maximum of $375 in tax savings.

When repaying a student loan, payments are applied to interest first, then principal. If payments have been deferred and interest has accrued during deferral, the amount of deductible interest may be high.

Education Planning

In addition to paying close attention to special issues related to education credits and deductions it would be prudent to make plans with all educational interests in mind.

Timing Techniques

Education credits have particular requirements that make timing an important part of claiming those credits. Taxpayers may be limited to a certain amount each year, and a limited number of years. The amount of the taxpayer's taxable income and tax owed will be another important factor. Dependency and other factors could also play a role in the planning process.

Prepayments

One way to accelerate qualifying expenses is to make allowable prepayments. Prepayments must apply to expenses incurred in the first three months of the subsequent year. You do not have to pay all of the tuition, and you could purchase some of the books in advance. This is a case where the preparer should be familiar with the client's family situation. To maximize the potential benefits it may be possible due to Treas. Reg. § 1.25A-5(e)(2) to pay for one semester in the prior year. If a child will be graduating in the following year, question them about the possibility of making prepayments to maximize the AOTC. This could also be beneficial if the student is receiving their undergraduate degree in December and attending graduate school the following year.

Alternate Years

One technique that may be useful is alternating years that you claim the AOTC and make prepayments in those years. For example, pay normally for Spring and Fall (2013), and prepay for the next Spring (2014) Then wait until the next year (2015) and do the same for Spring, Fall (2015), and Spring (2016). This can be useful if attendance is expected to last more than four years and expense amounts for two terms are less than $4,000.

Half-time At Least One Semester

The AOTC does require a student to be at least half-time at least one semester in the tax year, but once that requirement is met all qualifying expenses can be used. If a student attends the first semester and then takes a single class in each of the following semesters, all expenses can be used. Again, they also have the option of prepaying for a class beginning the following tax year (IRC § 25A(b)(2)(B)). Of course, it would not be very smart to prepay in a year when the student did not attend school.

While it is conventional to speak of credits in terms of semesters some institutions operate on a quarter system. Semesters are important because they generally cover at least one day in each of 5 months and can determine if the student is a full-time student for dependency reasons. The code for education credits does not include that limitation, only indicating that the student must be half-time during at least one academic period. Academic period is defined in Treas. Reg. § 1.25A-2(c) as "a quarter, semester, trimester, or other period of study as reasonably determined by an eligible educational institution." However, in cases where the credit is being claimed for a dependent, the student may need to be full-time for two quarters in order to meet the 5-month dependency requirement included in IRC § 152(f)(2).

Four Choice Years

Typically, school years span five taxable years, with the student only going to school one semester in each of the first and last years, but the AOTC can only be claimed for four years. If the student has limited expenses in some semesters she may wish to wait until years where qualifying expenses are greater, or a final semester when she has taxable income where she can take advantage of the nonrefundable portion of the AOTC.

In one common scenario the credit can be claimed for each of the first four tax years with the final school semester paid in advance. In another scenario the taxpayer could forego the credit in the first tax year (one semester), and claim the credit in the other four years with some graduate level expenses included in the year of graduation.

Graduate School Expenses

It is also possible that the AOTC can be used to pay for the first two semesters of graduate school. If a student graduates in May and then attends graduate school through the end of the year (summer and fall), all expenses for the year qualify for the AOTC. It may be better to forego the claim on the student's first (one-semester) school year so that they have the opportunity to claim the AOTC for this year. Form 8863 instructions are correct in indicating that the student cannot have earned a degree before the **start of the tax year.** Comments added to the final Treas. Reg. § 1.25A-3(d)(2) clarify that qualified expenses paid during the entire taxable year may be included in calculating the credit even if the student had completed their (then) first two years of undergraduate study during the year. Understanding the benefits to graduate students can be important since other benefits, such as the Pell grant, go away at the same time tuition costs increase.

Change of Plans

If necessary, it may be to the benefit of the taxpayer to amend tax returns to maximize the total benefit. Since some years can be amended it may be possible to make some adjustments there but the earlier years should be evaluated carefully since they will outside of the statue of limitations much sooner. For example, since amendments are limited to the past three years, the taxpayer may not want to waste the initial AOTC year on a smaller amount of credit.

Expiration Date

Don't forget the expiration date. With the current law scheduled to expire in 2017, and no surety that it will be extended, few years remain to allow for planning how and when to use the AOTC.

Coordinating Tax Credits With Other Benefits

Just as important as understanding the elective nature of traditional scholarships, federal grants, and AOTC qualified expenses, practitioners should be aware of how they potentially interact with educational costs such as room and board or computer technology. Whenever possible, practitioners should look for the best combination of benefits and work to coordinate them. This is particularly true if other sources are involved.

This information on other benefits is general in nature so taxpayers will need to do additional research and/or consult a personal financial planner before making plans with these instruments. Several benefits that can be used with education credits are retirement or savings related. Two are specifically for education while traditional or Roth IRAs could also be used for educational expenses. With the exception of traditional IRAs, each benefit discussed is after-tax, so that the contributions to these plans are not deductible. Additionally, if the benefit is not used for educational expenses the taxpayer may be subject to tax and/or penalties on distributions. Possible changes in these plans have also been in the news, so it would be wise to review current regulations on a regular basis.

In the article Tax Benefits for Education[48], John D. Zook suggests a hierarchy of benefits when considering qualified education expenses. Code sections have been added.

The Hierarchy of the Benefits

When considering [...] education-related exclusions, the taxpayer must consider the following hierarchy for them, as set out in the Code:

Qualified expenses will first be reduced by qualified scholarships, employer-provided educational assistance, and any other educational assistance that is excludible from income other than gifts, bequests, devises, or inheritances; (Sec. 25A(g)(2))

Any remaining qualified expenses are then permitted to be used for either the Hope credit (referred to as the American opportunity

48 http://www.thetaxadviser.com/issues/2010/jul/zook-jul10.html

tax credit in 2009 and 2010) or the lifetime learning credit; (Sec. 25A(g)(2))

Any remaining qualified expenses may then be allocated and claimed against distributions from Coverdell education savings accounts and qualified tuition plans; (Secs. 530(d)(2) and 529(c)(3) (B))

Any remaining qualified expenses may be used to exclude the interest from a qualified U.S. savings bond; (Sec. 135(d)(2)) and

Qualified expenses cannot be taken as a deduction if such expenses were taken as an exclusion or tax credit as enumerated above. (Sec. 222(c)(2))

It is true that grants and scholarships reduce expenses as an initial step, but you may have the ability to include some scholarships in income (not reducing expenses) and claim a credit or deduction instead.

After that you can choose to use any of the remaining benefits in any order. The important thing is to remember the concept of exclusivity, that expenses can be offset exclusively by only one benefit, or as Pub 970 frequently says "as long as the same expenses are not used for both benefits." Benefits claimed reduce available expenses.

In fact, benefits should often be claimed in a different order to maximize the benefits. For example, qualified expenses should generally not be reduced below $4,000 by elective scholarships when claiming AOTC.

Section 529/Coverdell accounts

In both Section 529 plans and Coverdell accounts contributions are not deductible but distributions are tax free if used for qualifying educational expenses. Although not deductible, lower-income taxpayers may be able to avoid taxation if their taxable income is lower. These plans are important because some expenses allowed are not qualifying expenses for education credits. Specifically, the terms in IRC § 529(e)(3)(B)(i) allow amounts withdrawn to pay for room and board expenses for students attending at least half-time. Thus, even though housing costs paid from a Coverdell or Section 529 can be tax-free; those amounts do not offset qualified expenses includable for the purpose of education credits. Publication 970 also confirms this by describing how to coordinate with other aid to maximize education credits.

Penalties

The law decrees that earnings distributed from Section 529 and Coverdell not used for educational expenses are taxed and penalized. Distributions, however, are not subject to a penalty provided the student receives a qualified scholarship that is used for qualifying expenses. The exclusion based on receipt of a scholarship applies only to the extent the distribution is not more than the scholarship, allowance, or payment (IRC §§ 530(d)(4)(B)(iii) and (2)(C)(i)(II)).

Additionally, the penalty does not apply if the distribution is included in income only because the qualified education expenses were taken into account in determining the American opportunity or lifetime learning credit (IRC § 530(d)(4)(B)(v)). The same rule applies to Section 529 distributions (IRC § 529(c)(6)).

Computers

One bonus of Coverdell is that certain computer technology purchases are now included in the list of **elementary** and **secondary** expenses that can be paid for by a qualified tuition program. The definition of qualified expenses in Section 530(e)(3)(A)(iii) includes computer technology, equipment, and Internet access if they are used by the beneficiary and family. Carefully note that the computer expense for family and beneficiary was a qualified **higher education** expense for 2009 or 2010 only, according to Section 529(e)(3)(A)(iii).

Otherwise, computer equipment is only a qualified expense for purposes of the AOTC if it is required.

Q7. **Does an expenditure for a computer qualify for the**

American opportunity tax credit?

A. Whether an expenditure for a computer qualifies for the credit depends on the facts. An expenditure for a computer would qualify for the credit if the computer is needed as a condition of enrollment or attendance at the educational institution.[49]

Include Section 529 Before Scholarships

Although distributions from both plans can be considered elective scholarships in the calculation of education credits it is better to include them in income before scholarships since only the earnings are taxable.

Distribution Timing

Timing is also important in regards to Section 529 and Coverdell accounts. Distributions can be used to cover calendar year expenses or expenses of the first three months of the following year. Distribution timing may be particularly important due to dependency support questions since distributions are considered support by the beneficiary.

IRAs

Don't confuse Roth IRAs and Section 529 accounts. They are taxed differently. Qualifying withdrawals from both are without penalty, but early withdrawals from an IRA that include earnings are still taxable. The only Roth IRA distribution that totally avoids taxation are qualified special purpose distributions which refer to qualified first-time home-buyer distributions (IRC §§ 408A(d)(2)(A)(iv), 408A(d)(5), and 72(t)(2)(F)).

Additionally, remember that different amounts are taxable or subject to penalty for each. Distributions from an IRA are from contributions first and then earnings whereas distributions from a Section 529 are pro-rated. If an IRA has $10,000 in contributions and $5,000 in

---

49 http://www.irs.gov/uac/American-Opportunity-Tax-Credit:-Questions-and-Answers, Accessed 3/25/2014.

earnings and a withdrawal is made for $5,000 for non-qualified expenses, there is no tax or penalty. If the same amounts are in a Section 529, one-third of the withdrawal will be subject to tax and penalty. If the withdrawal were for educational expenses, neither would be taxable, for different reasons.

If the full $15,000 is withdrawn, in both cases $5,000 would be subject to taxation and penalties. If withdrawn for educational expenses, the IRA would be taxed, but not the Section 529.

Penalty Avoidance

Individuals do have several options for early IRA withdrawals as provided in IRC § 72(t). By beginning distributions as part of a substantially equal payment plan (SEPP) they can avoid penalties (IRC § 72(t)(2)(A)(iv)) associated with early withdrawal. Such a plan must last for the life expectancy of the recipient, although modifications are governed by IRC § 72(t)(4). Generally, the payment can't change before the later of age 59½ or 5 years after the start of the SEPP. This could be a useful vehicle for funding a series of students' education. Similar opportunities are available for other retirement plans.

Another opportunity would be the use of funds that are associated with a first-time home-buyer. The taxpayer can use funds they might have used for purchasing a home for education and then take a distribution for the home. The definition of a first-time home-buyer is one that hasn't had ownership in a home in the prior 2 years (IRC § 72(t)(8)).

Special rules also exist for qualified employer retirement plans under IRC § 72(d) and related penalty exclusions for annuities are covered in IRC § 72(q).

Strategy

A primary strategy for the use of IRA and educational savings in paying education and claiming education credits would be to use amounts from tax-free aid (Section 529, Coverdell, etc.) to cover room and board, which qualify as tax-free under those code sections;

and if needed, use other scholarships as income to increase qualified expenses for the purposes of the education credits.

These are only a couple of things to consider when coordinating benefits. There are many other rules related to these accounts and it would be wise to examine all of the consequences, including their affect on financial aid qualifications. There are a number of books on Section 529 plans and taxpayers may also want to consult a personal financial planner if they are considering using savings plans to fund a significant amount of their education expenses.

Don't Forget the Other Tax Benefits

Education credits are just one source of funding for education and taxpayers should consider other benefits if they do not qualify for the credits. Since you generally cannot mix benefits for the same child a decision may need to be made based on which is most beneficial for each child. Since AOTC is the most generous and a portion of it is refundable, consider that before looking at other tax benefits, but don't waste one of the four years it is available on minimal qualified educational expenses.

Financial Advisors

One way to navigate the maze of educational opportunities and funding alternatives might be to employ a financial advisor. Depending on the type of education and the decisions that need to be made, an advisor can make you aware of options that you may not be aware of, and may be more up to date on those options. Savings plans and related regulations can change quickly without a lot of fanfare.

Be advised that not all financial advisors are well-versed in educational planning, and not all advisors are ethical. Credentialed advisors will have met strict testing and training requirements that can better insure they are credible. The most recognized credential in financial planning is the Certified Financial Planner (CFP) although there are others such as the Certified Financial Analyst (CFA) and AICPA's Personal Financial Specialist (PFS).

Additionally, many people find comfort in dealing with larger financial services companies such as Wells Fargo, that offer educational services.

Educational Planners

Alternately, advisors with some credential in educational planning would be appropriate. Education is but one frame in a larger financial picture. Often financial advisors are focused on investments, so they may not be what you want if you are not planning investments as a means of education funding.

If interested in educational planning in general, there are other organizations that can assist in applications. These advisors focus on education planning, and may not be good sources for financial advice. A Money article[50] on fraudulent college planning suggests limiting potential advisors that are members of either the National Association for College Admission Counseling (NACAC)[51], Independent Educational Consultants Association[52], or American Institute of Certified Educational Planners (AICEP).[53]

Initiated by IECA, AICEP offers the Certified Education Planner (CEP) credential which requires a masters degree, experience, and a written examination.

It is important to realize that some families may need to maintain a balance (or a combination) of advisors, having someone who has specific knowledge of educational planning, while also being able to keep the big picture in mind. Finally, it is as important to evaluate the advise given by an advisor as it is to selecting an advisor.

---

50 http://time.com/money/2793677/college-aid-dont-take-the-bait/
51 http://www.nacacnet.org/
52 http://www.iecaonline.com/
53 http://aicep.org/

The Future of Education Credits

The Future of Education Tax Credits is unknown. Although there has been much talk about making AOTC permanent, there is also discussion of changing other credits and deductions as a part of a package deal. While the AOTC is scheduled to expire in 2017 if nothing happens before then, prior legislation could drastically change circumstances.

In the past years various forces have presented options related to educational incentives, from both parties. Some have been from Congress as bills and as proposed budget adjustments, while the President has also proposed separate plans. The only actual legislation that has passed in the past few years is the requirement of a payee statement to claim the AOTC.

The future of education credits may not only affect the AOTC. The Lifetime Learning Credit could change or be eliminated, and the tuition deductions and other tax incentives like Section 529, Coverdell accounts, and even Pell grants could be affected by legislation. Before 2017, something is likely to change. Most proposals suggest eliminating some credits and enhancing the AOTC but there is no consensus on any element.

Congress

The last successful congressional action was in 2013[54] when the AOTC was extended until 2017. In June of 2014, the House passed H. R. 3393[55] that was anticipated to "consolidate four existing tax breaks... into one credit," but the bill was not taken up in the Senate. In it, the AOTC was enhanced to make $1,500 refundable, while the LLC and Tuition Deduction would have been eliminated.

When the committee first presented the bill, Accounting Today

---

54 http://www.ccdaily.com/Pages/Government/AOTC-extended-in-fiscal-cliff-plan.aspx
55 http://www.accountingtoday.com/news/government_news/house-committee-passes-education-tax-credit-simplification-bill-71081-1.html

reported on it and one of the comments on the article was that, "Anything that can be done to simplify this mess of incentives would be good."[56]

While some people lauded the efforts at simplification it was opposed by numerous college associations. Other comments on the Accounting Today report provided insight into the reason for those objections.

> *Simplification sounds great, but I agree with Rep. Sander Levin that by eliminating the Lifetime Learning Credit and the tuition deduction, life-time learners, graduate students, and undergrad students who do not complete their program in 4 years are left without any tax benefits to offset the growing cost of education. Marie Rosier, CPA MMR Tax www.mmrtax.com*

> *In other words, we are ELIMINATING all other education credits and simply keeping the current AOTC. First, not having any available credit for higher education after 4 years is the exact opposite of what needs to be done. Anyone who has to work while going to school will take longer than 4 years and this will just cause many to end up never graduating from college....*

> *Posted by: sbabi | July 25, 2014 7:37 AM*

> *This law is terrible. It doesn't address the needs of all students....*
> *Posted by: eastcoast ea | July 29, 2014 12:08 PM*

In a related action in 2015 budget proposals were presented that would eliminate guaranteed funding for Pell grants. Tax reform for educational incentives in the next few years seems inevitable. It does not appear that the issues will simply be extended though there will likely be some common elements that will not change.[57]

---

56 http://www.accountingtoday.com/news/government_news/house-committee-passes-education-tax-credit-simplification-bill-71081-1.html

57 http://www.washingtonpost.com/news/wonkblog/wp/2015/05/07/how-the-gop-house-republican-takes-aim-at-funding-for-college-students/

President

Earlier in 2015 President Obama proposed changes to educational incentives similar to H. R. 3393, which would also increase the refundable portion of AOTC and make it available for less than half-time students. It would also make it permanent and it would be good for 5 years instead of the current 4 years.[58] His proposal would also eliminate other tax breaks, including Section 529, Coverdell, interest deduction, and the tuition deduction. Within a week he backed down on Section 529 changes.

Schumer Proposal

Another voice in the call for reform of education credits in 2015 was U.S. Senator Charles E. Schumer, the author of the original AOTC bill. In March he proposed substantial changes to the credit.[59] His proposal would raise the annual amount to $3,000, with up to $1,500 refundable, but it would also make it available for unlimited years, and create a lifetime limit of 15,000. A part-time credit would be allowed for 30% of up to $10,000 in expenses which would also be refundable. It would remove the AOTC exclusion for drug offenses, and of course, omits the subsequently passed payee statement requirement. The Center for Law and Social Policy (CLASP) has compared Schumer's proposal with some other recent proposals.[60]

---

58 https://www.insidehighered.com/news/2015/01/17/president-obama-wants-overhaul-education-tax-credits-and-simply-taxes-pell
http://www.clasp.org/issues/postsecondary/in-focus/presidents-proposal-to-help-low-income-families-afford-college-through-improved-education-tax-credits

59 http://www.gpo.gov/fdsys/search/pagedetails.action?packageId=BILLS-114s699is
http://www.schumer.senate.gov/newsroom/press-releases/with-college-costs-soaring-schumer-launches-push-to-increase-and-expand-college-tuition-tax-credit-that-provides-much-needed-relief-for-upstate-ny-middle-class-families_new-bill-would-make-more-families-eligible-to-receive-tax-credit--grow-savings-to-up-to-3k-per-year

60 http://www.clasp.org/resources-and-publications/publication-1/Education-Tax-Credits-Refundability-Critical-to-Making-Credits-Helpful-to-Low-Income-Students-and-Families.pdf

Restrictions Proposed

In other legislation introduced in 2015 restrictions would be added to education tax credits to limit them to students that are legal residents. Diane Black introduced H. R. 2973 in July,

> *To amend the Internal Revenue Code of 1986 to require for purposes of education tax credit that the student be lawfully present and that the taxpayer provide the social security number of the student and the employer identification number of the educational institution, and for other purposes.*[61]

That legislation also proposes to require taxpayers to provide information supporting the student's legal status in order for the preparer to meet due diligence requirements.

AICPA

Outside of the government, the AICPA has made their own recommendation. The 2014 proposal recommends making AOTC 100% refundable and extending it to six years instead of four, pointing out that it takes most students six years to complete a degree. It would be without regard to undergraduate status. The credit would also be indexed to the cost of tuition rather than inflation.[62] Interestingly, the current law does have an adjustment for inflation, but it refers to the Hope Credit and not the AOTC (IRC § 25A(h)). It's impossible to tell what will be done with education credits or when legislation will be taken up to address incentives although some common threads in proposals include

- Increased refundable amounts
- Indexing to inflation or tuition costs
- Permanence
- Pell grant coordination
- Elimination of other credits, deductions

---

61 https://www.govtrack.us/congress/bills/114/hr2973/text
62 http://www.accountingtoday.com/news/aicpa-backs-education-tax-credits-simplification-70189-1.html

Conclusion

With all of the available education credits and deductions, it can be confusing to both taxpayers and preparers, and some simply dismiss education expenses if they don't know the available opportunity. With the currently available options, the most generous credit is the one that may be most overlooked. This is particularly true when the student is receiving a scholarship or other form of educational assistance. Both taxpayers and preparers need to better educated about educational incentives.

When clients mention educational expenses and then dismiss them because everything was covered by scholarships and other financial aid, ask to take a look and explain that they may be able to claim education credits of up to $2,500, especially if some of the expenses were paid with student loans, Pell grants, and some scholarships.

Even better, use the annual tax questionnaire to let clients know of the potential credit, even if they do not receive a 1098-T or are not out of pocket for any of the expenses. By understanding the regulations and the ability to treat scholarships as income, you can pleasantly surprise your clients. All that is needed is a little pre-season preparation, organization of client educational records, and a worksheet that calculates qualifying expenses used for the credit. Then see if that can be duplicated with prior year returns.

Whether clients can take advantage of tax credits or not, if educational expenses are anticipated in the near or distant future, discuss funding opportunities and potential tax savings of using Section 529, Coverdell, or some other tax-advantaged plan. Education expenses continue to rise along with the need for higher education so planning for them is more important than ever.

Education planning is also crucial since it has the potential of altering retirement plans.

Appendices

Appendix A: Explaining the AOTC

When I talk to a taxpayer about their return and the potential of claiming the American Opportunity Tax Credit (AOTC), they often are confused about it, especially if the AOTC involves including scholarships in income. I've struggled with how to explain it and continually expand or condense the explanation depending on how much I think they understand. In cases where the student and parent must coordinate their returns to get the biggest credit the explanation is even more critical since it must often be relayed to the third person.

This is my effort to outline the basics of the AOTC in an orderly and progressive way. The actual rules are more complex but this should help taxpayers understand what is happening. The first 5 include the basics of qualifying expenses, payments, and the amount of refundable or non-refundable credit.

The second half deals with scholarships mixed in, if some of the scholarships might be taxable or whether adjustments can be made to increase the credit amount.

1 The American Opportunity Tax Credit (AOTC) is available for the first $4,000 of qualifying educational expenses. The credit amount is calculated at 100% of the first $2,000 and 25% of the next $2,000.

2 Only 40% of the credit is refundable (max $1,000), and there are separate qualifying rules for the refundable part. The rest of it can only reduce the amount of tax paid.

3 Amounts paid in cash, credit, loans, or by third-parties are included in qualifying expenses. The amounts may be reported on a 1098-T but the taxpayer may need to verify the amounts with the student's financial account. A 1098-T is not required.

4 Qualifying expenses are amounts paid for tuition, books, and related expenses. Other expenses such as room and board don't count as qualifying expenses.

5 The AOTC is claimed on the return for which the student is being claimed as a dependent. If the student is claimed as a dependent on someone else's return the student cannot claim the AOTC.

6 If you receive scholarships that cover some of your expenses, they reduce the total amount of qualifying expenses.

Example 1: If you have qualifying expenses of $3,000 and scholarships of $2,000, the net amount of qualifying expenses available for claiming the AOTC is $1,000.

7 If scholarships are more than expenses, include the excess in income.
Example 2: If you have qualifying expenses of $3,000 and scholarships of $4,000, the amount of qualifying expenses is $0, and you have to include the additional $1,000 scholarship amount in income.

8 Some (not all!) scholarships can be included in income to increase your qualifying expenses. Pell grants can be treated that way.

Using example 1, if you have qualifying expenses of $3,000 and the $2,000 scholarship is a Pell grant you can include all of the scholarship in income and claim an AOTC on the full $3,000.

Using example 2, if you have qualifying expenses of $3,000 and the $4,000 scholarship is a Pell grant you have to include all $4,000 of the scholarship in income to claim the AOTC on the $3,000 expenses.

9 Scholarships are always the responsibility of the student. In order for the person claiming the dependency exemption (e.g. parent) to claim the maximum AOTC, the student may have to include scholarships in their income.

Using example 1 again, if the student includes the $2,000 in income, the parent can then claim the credit on all $3,000 in expenses. If the student is at the 10% tax bracket, it will cost $200, but the parent can reduce their tax by up to $2,250. If they don't owe tax to reduce they may still get $900.

10 Including scholarships in income doesn't always mean you have to pay tax on it. If your deductions and exemptions are more than your income, you won't have to pay income tax.

Appendix B: The Education Credit Campaign

This book and related articles on Switched Keys are a result of a personal campaign to educate preparers and the public about education credits. The urgency of the campaign is based on the fact that AOTC will end soon and that taxpayers need to be educated about scholarship inclusion. There are now other motivators, namely that next year a 1098-T will be required, so not receiving one will not only leave students uninformed, but soon after depriving them of the credit. It's hard for me to imagine the IRS/Treasury allowing this to happen.

Some tax professionals may not be concerned about the credit if their practice is limited to high-earning clients. Taxpayers with AGI over $180,000 do not qualify. I suspect that many CPAs do not limit their practice and they could see clients who do have educational expenses and the opportunity to claim the credit.

On the other hand, the laws and regulations are complex enough that minimally trained preparers may not understand how to maximize the credit. Yet, their clients with educational expenses are very likely to qualify for one of the credits.

If your practice involves educational incentives, you may also want to become involved in educating taxpayers, colleagues, institutions, and officials about the issues involved. In addition to articles posted on my blog, following are some of the items I used in trying to make others aware of educational incentives.

- Letter to Professionals
- Letter to Institutions
- News Releases
- Student Flyer

These items were created earlier in the year, so other issues need to be addressed in these letters considering the passage of HR 1295.

Tax Professional Letter

One of the ways I attempted to raise awareness of education credits was to send letters to local tax professionals. Following is an excerpt from one of those letters.

During the 2014 filing season I discovered that very few people are aware of the full potential of the American Opportunity Tax Credit (AOTC) and specifically the ability to include Pell grants and some scholarships in income to increase the AOTC. With this letter I am attempting to encourage more tax professionals to consider this valuable option provided by Treasury Reg. 1.25A-5(c)(3). If you understand this option but believe it involves too much work then you may find the tools I created to be helpful this tax season.

Although AOTC is discussed on many websites it isn't discussed in depth. After hours of searching the web, I have found little mention of coordinating AOTC and elective scholarships and grants. As a result, it seems plagued with misinformation and false assumptions. That misinformation has even been perpetuated by companies like H&R Block and Intuit, by tax software companies, and by financial aid departments of colleges and universities.

The AOTC is set to expire in 2017 and it would be unfortunate if people did not learn how to use it before it expires. The IRS cannot be faulted in failing to provide adequate exposure. The inclusion of grants and scholarships to increase AOTC has been in the regulations for years, has been included in Pub 970, and the Treasury Department, in a 2014 report to Congress, discussed the fact that so few take full advantage of the AOTC.

The Facts

1. By including Pell grants and some scholarships in income, you can maximize the amount of qualifying expenses for the credit. It's estimated that over 50% of students receive Pell grants, and it's possible that most of them would qualify for AOTC.

2. You don't need a 1098-T to file for AOTC. Institutions are not required to provide a 1098-T if financial aid covers expenses, but taxpayers often still qualify for the credit.

3. The 1098-T is often incorrect or incomplete. It will usually be necessary to get school account information from the clients to calculate the credits.

4. The AOTC is not just for the poor. Taxpayer MAGI need only be less than $90,000 (joint, $180,000). Even in the phase-out range, the first

$2000 of expenses will be valuable for the credit.

Tax software is great for many aspects of tax preparation, but it may not be so useful for calculating the AOTC. Using only a 1098-T, you probably don't have the information necessary to get correct amounts.

AOTC Toolkit

I've written a set of articles that explain education credits in more detail and provide tools that simplify the calculations. The articles explain how to gather information, tabulate qualifying expenses, and calculate the amounts for the tax return. To make it easier to evaluate the qualifications and calculate the credit, I've also prepared flowcharts and an AOTC worksheet. The toolkit includes:

- Education Credit Regulations: A discussion of the AOTC and the regulations that permit inclusion of grants and scholarships to increase qualifying expenses and the credit. Coordinating with other education programs is also discussed.

- Education Credit Preparation: Specific instructions for accessing and retrieving expense information from UT Tyler and TJC.

- Education Credit Calculations: One method for tabulating qualifying expenses and calculating the Credit. Includes the spreadsheet version of the AOTC worksheet.

- AOTC Flowcharts: The student qualification flowchart is the same as one published by the IRS. For the refundable credit test, instead of the IRS outline of those who do not qualify, I prepared a flowchart to identify those that do qualify. While the general consensus is that students over 18 and under 24 years of age do not themselves qualify for the refundable portion of the credit, there are exceptions that could easily be overlooked.

- AOTC Worksheet: The AOTC worksheet, unlike related IRS published worksheets, assists in maximizing the AOTC qualifying expenses and the taxable amount of scholarships. This pdf calculates the amounts automatically and includes examples from IRS publications and regulations.

The toolkit can be downloaded from

www.tylerhosting.com/EdCredit/

The Mission

I would like to encourage local tax accountants to gain a working knowledge of the full benefits of the AOTC, and so enable their clients to get this credit. Your clients may not be aware of their AOTC options, so your first step may be to include information in a client letter or with their annual tax organizer informing them that they may qualify for an education credit even if (1) grants and scholarships cover all of the cost or (2) they don't receive a 1098-T.

Secondly, I would like to see clients get the credit for any prior years for which they can amend their returns. While information on IRA conversions, Social Security strategies, trust techniques, and year-end strategies abound in trade publications and CAPE, advice on education planning and the AOTC is somewhat shallow. I hope the information I've collected will assist you in the upcoming tax season.

Letter to Institutions

Ask institutions to issue 1098-T even though not required.

I am a tax professional preparing for the 2015 filing season, and I'm writing to encourage <institution> to expand their release of 1098-Ts for students. I've written Enrollment Services concerning this and would like to solicit your support since you have the resources to verify the benefits of doing so. I understand that institutions are not required to issue 1098-T when financial aid covers all expenses, but it would often be to a student's advantage if they did. For those students for which a 1098-T is not required, an on-line version will meet that need with limited extra cost.

For example, a qualifying student or parent who receives $4000 or more in Pell grants and some other awards, and has that amount in educational expenses may be able to claim an American Opportunity Tax Credit (AOTC) of up to $1000, and an additional $1500 reduction in taxes by including those grants and scholarships in income. That is true whether or not they are out-of-pocket for any educational expenses.

While many people are aware of the AOTC, it is plagued by misinformation and false assumptions. That misinformation has even been perpetuated by companies like H&R Block and Intuit, and even some tax software companies.

IRS Publication 970 explains the inclusion of grants and scholarships in income to increase AOTC with several examples, and the actual regulations include examples of claiming the credit based on receipt of scholarships and grants. In a 2014 report to Congress even the Treasury Department discussed coordinating AOTC and Pell grants, releasing a fact sheet that explains how Pell grant recipients can get the credit.

> ... Most Pell Grant recipients should claim at least $2,000 in tuition and fees for the AOTC, even if that means allocating some of their scholarship money to living expenses and counting those amounts as taxable income.
>
> – Adam Looney, Deputy Assistant Secretary for Tax Analysis at the United States Department of the Treasury.

Many estimate that over half of students receive Pell grants so I suspect this affects quite a lot of students. Although receiving a 1098-T is not required, students and parents often do not realize that, and will fail to claim it. It would also be helpful if the University would provide general information about the ability to claim education credits even though they may receive grants and scholarships.

The University's assistance will help students and parents maximize their education resources with education credits. Even better, some of that refund money would likely end up back there.

P. S. I've also prepared an AOTC toolkit for tax professionals which explains the regulations in more detail. It can be downloaded from www.tylerhosting.com/EdCredit/. I would be happy to answer any questions you may have.

News releases

Following is an article on tax credits that may provide students information about tax credits that they may not be aware of. I will gladly answer any questions you may have.

Tax Credits for Students

Andrea is a 26 year old female that was unemployed for all of 2014 and decided to go back to school to complete her criminal justice degree in the fall. She registered in August, received a $1,000 scholarship, a $2,750 Pell grant, a $2,000 student loan, and had tuition and other educational expenses of $4,000. She had no kids, no job, and no house expenses. When it came time to file tax returns this year, she knew she didn't have to file because she didn't make any money, and her scholarship and Pell grant were tax free. She filed anyway because she knew she would get a $1,000 refund due to the American Opportunity Tax Credit.

Many taxpayers (even though they don't have to pay any taxes) are not aware of tax credits they might qualify for. An article in Accounting Today confirms that with a story of how the IRS is trying to encourage filing for tax refunds.

Two credits that may surprise students are the education credits and earned income credits. Both can be claimed even though you don't have to file a tax return. Some students may not realize they can claim education credits even though scholarships paid for most of their expenses. Tax-free scholarships can generally offset education expenses but in some cases students can include some or all of your scholarships and grants in income and then claim expenses paid for education. If the student is a dependent on their parents' return then their parents can claim. If you have little or no other income you may not have to pay any tax on the income, and still get the education credit.

This isn't a tax loophole either. The IRS issued treasury regulations in 2003, complete with examples, explaining how students can maximize their education credit this way. Those regulations are also published in IRS Publication 970 and have been recently promoted by the Treasury Department. In a 2014 report to Congress even the Treasury Department discussed coordinating AOTC and Pell grants, releasing a fact sheet that explains how Pell grant recipients can get the credit. Still, this permitted treatment is so little known that many tax preparers may not be aware of it.

The second credit often overlooked by new taxpayers is the earned income credit, although it has become more popular recently. If you work, even as a student worker, you could get a tax credit (refund) based on how much earnings you had during the year. Unlike the education credit, if you file a return with earned income and do not claim the earned income credit, the IRS may add that to your refund. They can't do that if you don't file a return. These are just two of the credits you could qualify for without having to pay taxes.

One other thing that many taxpayers are not aware of is that you can amend, or redo, tax returns. April 15 is the due date for filing your 2014 return but you can amend for three years after the due date. So when you file your 2014 return you can file/amend returns for 2011, 2012, and 2013 at the same time. That can be valuable if you haven't claimed the education credit for previous years.

If you don't want to pay someone to see if you can get one of these refunds, there are some free options for filing your tax returns. Volunteers in Tax Assistance (VITA) at the PATH office provides free tax assistance during tax season. VITA is sponsored by the IRS in coordination with charitable organizations and is staffed by volunteers certified by the IRS. Of course, if you want to consult a local tax professional, the IRS now has a list of credentialed tax pros at http://irs.treasury.gov/rpo/rpo.jsf.

All returns are different, so don't spend your money before you get it.

Depending on whether you filed or not, some of the things you'll need are: All W-2s, 1099s, 1098-Ts, and a list of other expenses. If you don't have a 1098-T, your school financial records can be used to calculate educational expenses paid to the university.

Other Actions

These are only a few things that can be done to better inform the public and your clients. Other actions that you may want to take include conducting seminars, providing training (CPE) for educational incentives, or distributing flyers to educate students.

Appendix C: TIGTA Finding

On May 5, 2015, the Treasury Inspector General for Tax Administration published a report that Billions of Dollars in Potentially Erroneous Education Credits Continue to Be Claimed for Ineligible Students and Institutions.[63] That report prompted congress to add restrictions to the law, but the report itself may be erroneous.

1098-T Deficiency

By far, the largest proportion of American Opportunity Tax Credit claims that appear to be erroneous did not have an associated Form 1098-T at all. However, much of the suspected fraud may be due to the fact that institutions are not always required to provide one, even though the taxpayer qualifies for the credit.

The report indicated that

> Educational institutions are required to provide a Form 1098-T to students who attend their institution and file a copy of Form 1098-T with the IRS. The Form 1098-T provides the name and Employer Identification Number (EIN) of the institution, the name and Taxpayer Identification Number of the student who attended, and information on whether the student attended half-time or was a graduate student.

It appears that TIGTA did not consider the regulations that limit the number of students a 1098-T is issued to. If scholarships exceed expenses, however, institutions generally do not issue a 1098-T. The report did not even contain the word "scholarship".

Reasons

There are many reasons for not receiving a 1098-T.

- Expenses and scholarships are mismatched on the 1098-T. All scholarships and grants are reported on the 1098-T whether for qualified or non-qualified expenses, but only qualified expenses are reported on the 1098-T. The reporting exception

---

63 https://www.treasury.gov/tigta/auditreports/2015reports/201540027fr.pdf

allowed to institution relies on this mismatched comparison.

- The reported amounts are often misaligned chronologically. The institution has the option of reporting amounts paid or amounts billed. Very often the amounts shown as billed in the current year are for a term in the following tax year, while scholarships are not being provided until that following year. For example, the bill for the Spring semester may be dated in December, while the payment doesn't occur until January.

- Not all qualified expenses appear on a 1098-T. In the case of the American Opportunity Tax Credit, students could incur qualified expenses that are not reported on a 1098-T. For example, books purchased outside of the institution are qualified expenses that can be used to claim the credit.

- Some scholarships and grants can be included in income. Treas. Reg. § 1.25A-5 allows taxpayers to include certain scholarships and grants in income to increase the education credit. Pell grants are included in this category. This may have been in response to instructions in the bill (ARRA) that created the American Opportunity Credit and has been promoted by the IRS on several occasions.

In the report, TIGTA estimated $19 billion in education credit claims for 2012, and suggested $5.6 billion in potential fraud, with $3.2 billion due to not having a 1098-T on file. That's almost 30% in potential fraud according to TIGTA.

The $3.2 billion due to not having a 1098-T represents 2.2 million students. Since Pell grants often cover qualified expenses, and the requirement to provide a 1098-T, Pell grants may be the biggest single reason for the TIGTA discrepancy.

Analysis

Although the amounts are sketchy at times, we can estimate the amount of potentially valid tax credit claims due to Pell grants, claims that may not have an associated 1098-T.

Enrollment

Enrollment in college has been reported to be almost 21 million[64], although that number appears to be enrollment for the year, instead of a total number of students that attended at any time during the year.

Since freshman and seniors generally only attend half-year we could assume an additional 5 million, but sticking with the more conservative 21 million students we can safely estimate how much could be claimed based on Pell.

Note: Footnote 16 of the TIGTA report indicates receipt of 28.2 million 1098-Ts which is comparable with possible enrollment numbers, so it appears that the IRS receives a 1098-T for all students even though the student does not receive one. Since the student does not report the EIN of the institution unless he receives a 1098-T he would be considered filing without one.

Awards

The College Board reports 9.4 million recipients of $34.5 billion in Pell grants[65], with an average grant amount of $3685 for the 2011/2012 school year. If you factor in need-based scholarships that accompany the grant, the financial aid total will likely offset qualified expenses for many students and they would not receive a 1098-T.

If, for simplicity, we ignore other aid and assume all students could claim credit based on Pell grants, we can estimate how much they could receive. Because of income qualifications for the Pell grant, in most cases, Pell recipients would not be subject to phaseout rules.

Calculation

With an average grant of $3,685, the average credit would be $2000 + 421 (25% of 1685) = $2421 per student, or a total of $22.7 billion in

---

64 http://nces.ed.gov/programs/digest/d13/tables/dt13_303.10.asp
65 http://media.collegeboard.com/digitalServices/pdf/advocacy/policycent er/advocacy-rethinking-pell-grants-report.pdf

claims. That's only for the 9.4 million recipients. Add another 11 million students who either pay in cash or have other types of financial aid and the amount could approach $40 billion and the actual claims of $19 billion may be a bargain. If the credit is limited to the refundable portion (40%), that is still a significant amount.

The problems with 1098-T statements do not stop with the lack of receipt. The TIGTA also classified graduate student classification as another indicator of erroneous claims. The 1098-T contains a checkbox to indicate Graduate School status but the instructions are not clear on when that status is determined. Absent other instructions, most institutions will likely indicate that status based on the end of the year, although the credit requirements indicate that the graduate school test is at the beginning of the year (IRC § 25A(b)(2)(C)).

Congressional Action

Responding to the report in knee-jerk fashion, congress passed a law requiring taxpayers to have a 1098-T in order to claim the AOTC, LLC, and tuition deductions. In response to that law I suspect the IRS will now require institutions to provide the 1098-T to all students. The concern of TIGTA is the loss of funds, but if 1098-Ts will be required in all cases, and institutions are required to provide them, there may be a significant increase in credit claims in the future. Of course, that's only if taxpayers were better informed about education credits.

It will be a while before finding that out, though. The 2015 report was for 2012 so a subsequent report for 2015 claims would likely be delayed until after 2017, the last year of the AOTC as it now stands.

Appendix D: Recommendation Letter on IRC § 25A(g)(8)

On June 29, 2015, Congress passed a law which would require taxpayers to have a payee statement for educational expenses in order to claim an education credit. Current regulations, however, allow institutions to limit those statements to students with expenses greater than scholarships. Without changes in the regulations this will have the effect of depriving some taxpayers of the credit based solely on the institutions actions. This is my letter to the IRS encouraging prompt action on this matter.

July 27, 2015

The Honorable John A. Koskinen
Commissioner
Internal Revenue Service
1111 Constitution Avenue, NW
Washington, DC 20224

Ms. Janet McCubbin
Director of Individual Taxation
Department of the Treasury
1500 Pennsylvania Avenue NW, Room 4115
Washington, DC 20220

Mr. W. Adam Looney
Deputy Assistant Secretary (Tax Analysis)
Department of the Treasury
1500 Pennsylvania Avenue NW, Room 4115
Washington, DC 20220

Ms. Nina E. Olson
National Taxpayer Advocate
Internal Revenue Service
1111 Constitution Avenue, NW
Washington, DC 20224

Re: Adverse effect of changes in IRC § 25A by H.R. 1295 on the ability of taxpayers to claim education credits when considering current institution reporting requirements

Dear Messrs. Koskinen and Looney, and Mmes. McCubbin and Olson:

On June 29, 2015 Congress passed H.R. 1295 which, among other things, requires taxpayers to have a valid information form (1098-T) in order to claim an education credit or deduction. The new IRC § 25A(g)(8) states:

> Except as otherwise provided by the Secretary, no credit shall be allowed under this section unless the taxpayer receives a statement

furnished under section 6050S(d) which contains all of the information required by paragraph (2) thereof.

A similar requirements is imposed for taxpayers claiming a tuition deduction. While this law is a step toward curbing some amount of education credit fraud, with current treasury regulations in place for information reporting and the exceptions allowed, many qualified taxpayers will be deprived of the ability to claim education credits as a result.

Background

Prior to the passage of this bill, taxpayers could claim education credits based on qualified expenses incurred. Treasury regulations detail the requirements for the credit in Treas. Reg. § 1.25A-1 through 1.25A-5. Institutional reporting requirements are outlined in Treas. Reg. § 1.6060S-1. While the law required institutions to provide information reports (for which the IRS designed the 1098-T), the regulations included some significant exceptions. Currently Treas. Reg. § 1.6050S-1(a)(2)(iii) allows institutions to forgo the submission of information reports (1098-T) when scholarships are greater than expenses.

The information reporting requirements of this section do not apply with respect to any individual whose qualified tuition and related expenses are waived in their entirety or are paid entirely with scholarships.

In the past this lack of reporting has left many taxpayers unaware of their qualifications for the education credit. Consequently, I've attempted to educate taxpayers and institutions of the need to provide information returns for all students. Still, taxpayers could still claim the credit based on their own documentation and as reflected in college student records.

As of the effective date of H.R. 1295 taxpayers will now be required to have a 1098-T. Although the change will help to identify and prevent education credit fraud it is likely that many will now be deprived of the credit.

Change Analysis

The requirements imposed by H.R. 1295 requiring taxpayers to have a valid information form (1098-T) is not consistent with the reporting exceptions currently in place. Institutions are not required to provide the 1098-T when scholarships exceed expenses but it is likely that with the new reporting requirement that taxpayers will be deprived of the credit. Treasury regulations need to be reconciled with the new law for the following reasons:

- **1098-T Information is often not complete and may not be accurate.** The 1098-T does not indicate qualifications for the credit. It is well known by tax professionals that 1098-T reporting must be verified with actual expenses and payments. Amounts on a 1098-T cannot be simply transferred to an education credit claim.
- **Expenses and scholarships are mismatched on the 1098-T.** All scholarships and grants are reported on the 1098-T whether for qualified or non-qualified expenses, but only qualified expenses are reported on the 1098-T. The reporting exception allowed to institution relies on this mismatched comparison.
- **The reported amounts are often misaligned chronologically.** The institution has the option of reporting amounts paid or amounts billed. Very often the amounts shown as billed in the current year are for a term in the following tax year, while scholarships are not being provided until that following year. For example, the bill for the Spring semester may be dated in December, while the payment doesn't occur until January.
- **Not all qualified expenses appear on a 1098-T.** In the case of the American Opportunity Tax Credit, students could incur qualified expenses that are not reported on a 1098-T. For example, books purchased outside of the institution are qualified expenses that can be used to claim the credit.
- **Some scholarships and grants can be included in income.** Treas. Reg. § 1.25A-5 allows taxpayers to include certain scholarships and grants in income to increase the education credit. Pell grants are included in this category. This may have been in response to instructions in the bill (ARRA) that created the American Opportunity Credit and has been promoted by the IRS on several occasions. The reverse side of the 2015 1098-T now includes this tip:

    TIP. You may be able to increase the combined value of an education credit and certain educational assistance (including Pell Grants) if the student includes some or all of the educational assistance in income in the year it is received. For details, see Pub. 970.

    Some examples of treating scholarships as income in Publications 970 (Examples 3, 4) and Treas. Reg. § 1.25A (Example 4) include cases where scholarships exceed reported qualified expenses.

In any of these cases, scholarships could appear to offset the qualified expenses. If institutions do not provide a 1098-T in these cases, which appears very common, the taxpayer will now be denied the credit. That would have the effect of depriving the neediest taxpayers for which the initial law was designed.

Recommendation

I would like to recommend that regulations be modified to require institutions to issue 1098-T for all students without the exception provided in Treas. Reg. § 6050S-1(a)(2)(iii). There are other possible remedies as the new law does allow the Secretary to make other provisions in applying IRC § 25A(8)(g) but this seems to be the simplest one. This would also provide awareness to taxpayers of potential tax benefits that has been lacking in the past.

Because institutions need time to modify computer systems used to generate the information reports it is important that this issue be considered promptly. Additionally I would recommend that regulations be added to require an institution to issue a 1098-T to students on request upon submission of a valid TIN or if a 1098-T was not already provided for any other reason for any tax year.

Benefits

There are other benefits of requiring institutions to provide information reports (1098-T) to all students. More complete reporting will provide a better picture of the cost and benefits of education credits and possible education credit fraud. The very high estimate of education credit fraud as recently presented by the Treasury Inspector General for Tax Administration is likely due to the fact that claims do not match 1098-Ts. That report identifies two million claims without 1098-T but there is no information provided for how many qualifying taxpayers do not receive that form solely due to Treas. Reg. § 1.6050S-1(a)(2)(iii). That report indicated

> *The IRS can use the Form 1098-T to verify that a student claiming an education credit attended an eligible educational institution or attended for the required period of time.*

In reality, the IRS CANNOT use the form as verification where institutions are not required to provide it.

Conclusion

In addition to being an Enrolled Agent I've volunteered with tax assistance agencies like VITA and Tax-Aide for several years. As a tax preparer there I saw many low-income taxpayers that qualified for education credits who did not receive a 1098-T from their college. We verified qualifications and then calculated the credit based on student records from the college. Many of them were pleasantly surprised to learn they could receive this credit.

Ignorance of the credit among taxpayers was so common that I wrote a guide on the subject of education credits. While I will need to modify one of the premises of the book (that a 1098-T was not required), I would like to see that these low-income taxpayers are not deprived of the credit simply because institutions are not required to send them a 1098-T. Requiring institutions to issue this form to all students will also aid in educating taxpayers about the qualifications for the credit.

I appreciate the opportunity to write concerning this issue and I'm confident that the taxpayers I assist will also be thankful for your consideration of this matter. If you have any questions, [....].

Sincerely,

Dana Bell, EA

Index

About the Author

Dana Bell is a graduate of the University of Texas at Tyler. He has degrees in Accounting and Computer Information Systems, and received his Enrolled Agent designation in 2014. He is also working toward CPA certification. During tax season he enjoys volunteering with VITA and Tax-aide.

In addition to writing about tax accounting and business concerns, Dana is a computer programmer, website developer and host, database guru, and graphic designer. His favorite pastimes include disc golf, photography, chess, and Scrabble™.

Professional and Social Media

LinkedIn: https://www.linkedin.com/in/dbell154/

Switched Keys (blog): http://www.tylerhosting.com/b2e/

Resume: http://www.tylerhosting.com/dbell/resume/

Personal Site: http://www.tylerhosting.com/dbell/

FaceBook: http://www.facebook.com/dbell154/

Twitter: http://www.twitter.com/dbell154/

LibraryThing: http://www.librarything.com/profile/dbell154/

Smashwords:
https://www.smashwords.com/profile/view/dbell154/